THE MEANING OF
MANNERISM

THE MEANING OF
MANNERISM

EDITED BY
FRANKLIN W. ROBINSON
AND
STEPHEN G. NICHOLS, JR.

UNIVERSITY PRESS OF NEW ENGLAND
HANOVER, NEW HAMPSHIRE 1972

International Standard Book Number: 0-87451-068-6
Library of Congress Catalog Card Number: 71-189512

Design and Typography by Elizabeth Hickler
Printed in the United States of America

CONTENTS

FOREWORD

THE substance of this book is a series of six papers that were read at the New England Renaissance Conference, sponsored by the New England Renaissance Society and held at Dartmouth College, October 3 and 4, 1970. In addition to the presentation of papers, the conference had two especially installed exhibitions: "Scholar's Choice: The Collection of Benjamin Rowland, Jr.," in the Jaffe-Friede Gallery of the Hopkins Center, and an exhibition of incunabula and other rare books in the Dartmouth College collection, in the Rare Book Room, Baker Library. On October 3, Benjamin Rowland, Jr., professor of fine arts, Harvard University, gave a gallery talk on the exhibition of his collection; and I Dilettanti of Harvard University, under the direction of Anthony Newcomb, presented a concert of late sixteenth-century madrigals from the Este and Gonzaga Courts.

We are grateful to the New England Renaissance Society for making this occasion possible and to the contributors to this volume for their distinguished papers. Mrs. Mireille Kofler kindly typed the manuscript. The University Press of New England has given great help and encouragement at every stage of the project.

F.W.R.
S.G.N., Jr.

Hanover, New Hampshire
September, 1971

THE MEANING OF
MANNERISM

INTRODUCTION

THE first question to be answered in a book such as this is, Why should it be published? Why preserve such a diverse collection of essays, from one symposium, to be sure, but spanning so many different fields? Clearly, the individual essays deserve a wider audience; but why together within one volume?

Such questions go to the heart of the problem posed in the title of the symposium and wrestled with by the contributors. Mannerism is a complex phenomenon, to say the least. There is little agreement on any aspect of it: Is *mannerism* synonymous with the Italian *maniera*, or is it a style embracing a variety of phenomena? If it is the latter, is it a period style, or are we justified in finding "mannerist" aspects to works of art throughout history, and not just in the sixteenth century? Should the term be used at all or, at best, only suggestively and not with any precise definition? Some scholars maintain the term should be used only in referring to visual works of art, or even just to painting and prints, while others would apply it to all the arts and even to social phenomena. There is no question, then, that serious debate on mannerism is needed; this fact, in itself, would justify the present volume.

Further, as scholars sometimes complain, the term *mannerism* is applied to many fields by the specialist in only one. While there may be ultimate value in *paragone* of the arts, it is good, for once, to have separate attacks on the problem, made by scholars working in their own fields, but jostling one another and even denying that they *should* be neighbors.

Beyond these considerations, general problems of methodology are presented by this collection. These essays use different approaches, not only to the description of particular styles, but also to the concept of style itself, not only to *how* the arts relate to each other, but also to *whether* they do at all. We regret the absence of contributions from political and social historians, not to speak of historians of science, economics, and demography. Indeed, perhaps we also need enlightenment from the history of costume and the history of manners (in the modern sense). This book raises, implicitly and sometimes explicitly, a fundamental question: Is it possible—or desirable—to have valid insights and interpretations of an interdisciplinary nature?

In the individual essays the approaches are bewildering, or fruitful, in their variety, depending on the point of view. For example, Greene takes one work of art that "realizes and intensifies and . . . authenticates the diffused tendencies of its past tradition" and through that work, a poem, comes to a general insight about the nature of mannerism—that it is bound up with the periphrase,

3

the circumlocution. Although mannerism "risks turning style into a scandal" and
the reader sometimes feels a "sense of satiety," there is, for Greene, a deeper
power and sense of beauty embedded in, and expressed by, the circumlocutions
and other elements of the style: "Even the most insistent style is docile enough,
in the hands of a master, to support the burden of expression."

Palisca also approaches the problem of mannerism through the analysis of a
single work. Although he expresses hesitation about generalizing from one art
to another and even about accepting the word *mannerism* at all, he shows the
prevalence in contemporary music of gesture and ornament, the evaded cadence
—a style that is elegant, artful, unexpected, and clever. Complex devices in the
music are described by contemporary writers in terms borrowed from rhetoric,
such as *anadiplosis* and *anaphora*. Thus, almost against their will scholars are
forced to move from one art to another or even to another whole segment of
the social life of the age. In Edgerton's essay on executions in the sixteenth century and their reflection in paintings, prints, and drawings, the very attitudes of
the condemned toward public death and of the crowds toward this spectacle
are seen as expressions of a mannerist esthetic. Decorum and decapitation,
violence and style, are closely linked in the sixteenth-century mind. Edgerton
points out that the brotherhood that comforted condemned men, accompanied
them to their execution, and buried them made their church in Rome, San
Giovanni Decollato, the repository of some of the most important Italian mannerist paintings, several of them directly related to the brotherhood's grim mission. Michelangelo was only the most famous of the several distinguished artists
to belong to it.

In contrast, Mirollo and Zerner concentrate, not so much on individual works
of art as on a methodological approach to the whole subject. They ask: What
does mannerism mean? What did it mean in the sixteenth century? What has
it meant to scholars throughout the twentieth century? What should it mean
today? Mirollo identifies two general tendencies in the definition of the phenomenon, that of *Angst* mannerism, in which the pain, the disturbances, the deform-
ations of many sixteenth-century works are taken as the hallmark of the style;
and that of mannerism as the "stylish style," a style without profound spritual
or emotional content or impact. He also suggests an alternative approach that
does not completely reject the conclusions of either of these tendencies. In fact,
he suggests that a variety of motives may explain why a particular artist becomes
mannerist at one moment in his career or another. He further warns that literary
mannerism should be defined in terms of literary criticism, rather than in terms
of the criticism of some other art. Finally, Mirollo proposes that the definition
should be narrowed down and that "mannered" aspects of much of contemporary literature should be excluded from the discussion. He also puts forward

his own view that mannerist art, on the whole, is parasitic and parodic in nature, a reaction to, a play against, a High Renaissance or classical norm.

Zerner, too, reviews the literature on the concept of mannerism, primarily from the viewpoint of an art historian, and finally comes to a definition, not wholly different from Dvořák's *Angst* mannerism, but arrived at through a wide-ranging study of sources, commentaries, and original works. Zerner asserts that the refinement and elegance of the "stylish style" can exist, as in Parmigianino's *Madonna of the Long Neck,* alongside of a vision of spiritual beauty and seriousness. Alienation is a key aspect of this view of mannerism. "As they became conventional and institutionalized, the charged forms and figures, no longer attached to particular feelings, emotions, or situations, became expressive of a communal subconsciousness. . . . The rhetorical exaggeration, the emptiness of expressive poses, which are playful on one level, also reveal an underlying unrest, an unadmitted torment." Zerner sees in these works "a strangely troubling absurdity" in which, in the end, "amusement becomes a pretext and a mask for seriousness." And perhaps the need to have such pretexts and masks for pain, that excessive sensitivity, is an important part of that pain in itself.

This volume of speculation and conjecture, definition and redefinition, ends with Nash's illustrated essay on printing; it seems appropriate to have as a conclusion a short dialogue from the sixteenth century that is, to be sure, concerned with words, but only in the most practical manner, with printing them.

Is the concept of mannerism a useful one for us today? Why the new interest in, and respectability for, it now? Zerner points out that "the justification of the forms in the *maniera* was exterior to the context in which they were used"; this is true even for the form of many mannerist objects whose reason for being is supposedly functional. There are sixteenth-century daggers that are murderous in appearance but too delicate to be grasped with any strength, ewers out of which nothing can be poured, frames that are larger and more elaborate than the paintings they were meant to surround. This indirection, this sliding away from a direct confrontation with reality, indeed, this distrust of reality and of the identity of reality and appearance—whether in specific devices like the evaded cadence and the periphrase and the stylized execution or in such evaluations as parasitic and parodic or a symptom of a deep alienation—is not unique to the sixteenth century. In this reaction against the classical norm and the equilibrium of the High Renaissance, against the concept of the wholeness of body and spirit, against the unquestioned belief in the possibility of health and sanity—in this limited sense, are we not all mannerists?

No definition of a style can be used to characterize all the works produced within a period or even within the same art. No definition can encompass all the complex and contradictory elements of all the individual works that are considered examples of that style. Such a definition is only an arrow pointing at certain tendencies more prevalent in this group of works than in most other works of the time, or earlier or later. This collection hopes to provide a few of these arrows.

F.W.R.

I

THE MANNERED AND THE MANNERIST
IN LATE RENAISSANCE LITERATURE

James V. Mirollo

FROM the viewpoint of the literary historian and critic, the subject of this symposium could hardly be more piquant. For if there is one question above all others—and there *are* others, as I shall mention later—that arises whenever the word *mannerism* is used in literary discussion, it is: "What does it mean?" Now one may answer that question in at least three important and useful ways: one may critically review the numerous articles and books that proffer theories about the concept; or one may assume the correctness of one theory and proceed to demonstrate its appropriateness to one or more literary works or authors; or, finally, one may pretend not to harbor even a tenuous hypothesis and simply analyze a group of poems or plays or fictions in search of a different or unique underlying poetic—which may turn out to have a kind of relationship to the esthetics of mannerist art. All three of these methods may contribute something to our understanding of the concept of mannerism, despite their obvious ultimate insufficiencies; but to attempt the second or third without at least acknowledging the disturbing results that would be produced by the first, may, at this point in our progress, smack of evasion of duty. The notion of a literary mannerism is so vague and confused, so hopelessly stalled at a quite primitive stage of discussion (as Professor Greene notes in the following essay), that one may well tremble at the prospect of making another contribution to the chaos. Thus, while it would be more entertaining for me, and possibly for the reader, if I were to devote all of this paper to commentary on certain sixteenth-century or early seventeenth-century literary works—commentary intended to prove not only that there *is* a literary mannerism but also that I have *the key* to its meaning—I would certainly run the risk of stirring in my reader the second question most frequently heard in literary debate, that is, "Whose mannerism?" I therefore propose, first, to treat candidly certain painful aspects of *l'état présent* of the question and, second, to suggest some ways out of the mess we are in, with due reference to a few literary works I regard as crucial if we are to persuade ourselves, the would-be believers, as well as the many, many non-believers, that we are

7

possibly on the right track when we spend our time on, or vex our brains about, this blessed mannerism.

A fundamental requirement—one that has not yet been fully met by literary scholars entranced with our subject—is a thorough analytical survey of what has, in fact, been said about literary mannerism during the fifty years or so since the question was first raised in Germany (where else?) by art historians like Werner Weisbach and Max Dvořák.[1] Some attempts have been made, notably by Alan M. Boase, Georg Weise, Eugenio Battisti, and Riccardo Scrivano, to do the job, but these have been flawed in one way or another, and in any event none has matched in scope and clarity René Wellek's masterly treatment of the controversy over the baroque.[2] What *has* happened is that several literary critics (including in this country, significantly enough, a bright Yale undergraduate) have determined upon a theory of literary mannerism—or borrowed it from one of the art historians who has "made it" in paperback—and then applied it to works hitherto thought to be exemplary of late Renaissance or baroque style.[3] (It would seem that at least part of the attraction of such criticism is the opportunity it tantalizingly offers of saying something fresh or original about exhausted works.) And they have sprung these critiques on their fellow scholars, still reeling from the shock of revisionism precipitated by the baroque and just barely beginning to accept the notion that baroque may, after all, mean something sensible and useful. Then, of course, there are our colleagues among the art historians or social historians or just plain historians—the names of Frederick B. Artz, Wylie Sypher, Arnold Hauser, and John Shearman come readily to mind—who have felt obliged to broaden the concept of mannerism in the arts by bringing in analogues from literature, with varying degrees of success, to put it charitably, and with the outcome, though not always the stated purpose, the positing of an intervening style between Renaissance and baroque, if not a new, and still another, comprehensive period in European culture.[4]

Now lest my general sense of unease about these various attempts at elucidation of a literary mannerism suggest the recalcitrance of the nonbeliever, the perpetual deplorer of facile *paragoni* of the arts, I should state at once that on the matter of the value and utility of comparing the arts I am as sanguine as a Baldassare Castiglione or a Lodovico Dolce, even when I suspect that they did it much better than we do. No student of the period under discussion can ignore the fact that *paragone* was really an esthetic donné of the time, something genuinely believed in and therefore influential on the way artists thought and worked, and not merely a literary aria, full of decorative trills, that one performed on occasion for an appreciative audience—although it could be that, too. (To the continuing skeptics among my literary colleagues, I can do no more than recommend the defiance of Lessing, as well as Wellek and Warren, to be found in Mario Praz's *Mnemosyne,* which should settle the question for all

but the hopelessly prejudiced defenders of a "purity" of the literary medium.[5])
To say, then, that the establishing of a concept of literary mannerism is bogged
down in serious difficulties is not to say we don't need it.—The third question
literary scholars often ask about the meaning of mannerism is, Who needs it?—I
think it urgent, therefore, to assert briefly, before pointing to specific remedies
for those difficulties, just why we do need the concept of mannerism in our
study of the English and Continental literatures of the period embracing most
of the sixteenth and a portion of the seventeenth century.

For general arguments in favor of a concept of literary mannerism we can
do no better than to glance at the positive side of the history of the baroque. One
of its most inspired interpreters, Jean Rousset, aptly reminds us of the benefits
that have accrued from employing the concept of the baroque as an instrument
of research and criticism.[6] Several interesting and important authors have been
rediscovered and revaluated—and others, we might add, rehabilitated—and at
the same time we have taken another look at familiar authors and works, with
some fresh insights the bonus for our labors. Whatever may be said of the
thousand snares that attend these benefits, it is still as a general principle very
worthwhile for literary scholars occasionally to look at their subject in the light
emanating from other disciplines, especially art history and especially when the
period in question is one in which the various arts tended to be treated as differing but related offspring of the same human needs and capacities, to be measured
by the same esthetic yardstick—as I indicated above in regard to the literary
exercise known as the *paragone*.

More specifically, we must admit the maps of the European literary landscape
before the invasion of the concepts of baroque and mannerism were hardly satisfactory. The prime example in English literary history is the gradual recognition of the woeful inadequacy of such labels as *metaphysical, Ramism,* and *Tribe
of Ben,* as recent writings by Martz, Warnke, and Summers, each in its own
way, clearly demonstrate.[7] In truth, we have long been aware that the label
Renaissance does not quite account for literary developments in Italy after the
mid-sixteenth century, in France after the Pléiade, and in Spain after Garcilaso
and Boscán (although many students of Spanish literature arrived at this insight
earlier than their colleagues, some even doubting the existence of a Spanish
Renaissance at all). At the end of the last century it was fashionable among
European comparatists to link John Lyly, Giambattista Marino, and Luis de
Góngora in an absurd formulation of a Europe-wide decadence in literary
taste.[8] In our own time, too, we have had formulations of *counter-Renaissances*
to encompass the known and recognizable divergencies in literary currents, these
being explained in terms of reaction and opposition to Renaissance ideology
spurred by religious and political crisis.[9] The prime examples here, of course, are
the thought and prose styles of Machiavelli and Montaigne.

Many of us are old enough, or have read back far enough, to remember when the literature of the Renaissance was a vast panorama beginning with Dante and ending with Milton and Calderón. Looked at from this perspective, the discussion of mannerism may be considered an inevitable, and necessary, outgrowth of continuing uncertainty about the scope, limits, and content of the concept of the Renaissance, with concomitant speculation about its esthetic assumptions and their stylistic manifestations. The so-called revolt of the medievalists and the onslaught of the baroque partisans having led the way in defining more precisely what we mean by *Renaissance,* the concept has been subjected to closer inspection and more minute analysis.[10] It is no accident that, as we have reached a near consensus about the baroque—which emphasizes its basic healthiness, its hearty recapitulation in more emphatic terms of Renaissance esthetic standards, its emotional realism, its drama and energy in reaction to alleged mannerist preciosity and complexity—all of the "negative" features of baroque art and literature, once used to condemn it, have been transferred to mannerism to be revaluated in its context.[11] And, as we shall see, the concept of mannerism, too, is now being fragmented, as it, too, undergoes exhaustive probing. It is also no accident that mannerism is being investigated by art and literary historians at the same time as other historians are looking with a fresh eye at the long-simmering problem of the "Late Italian Renaissance," to which Eric Cochrane has devoted a study with precisely that title.[12] In all this discussion of post-, counter-, and late Renaissances there must surely emerge a consensus in which the mannerist style in art and literature must have its place, unless we wish to take the extreme position that styles in the arts bear no relationship, chronologically or substantively, to their cultural environment—the other extreme, that they are inextricably tied to, and fully explainable in terms of, that environment, being the more popular and therefore the more dangerous of the two positions.

Now admittedly, at first or even second sight, all of this debate is discouraging. How can one get a scholarly grip on it? How can it be taught? How can it be set forth in textbooks, which by their nature require clear and convenient schemes? [13] One answer is to avoid critical and historical absolutism and instead, as Rousset argues, to employ such concepts as mannerism and baroque as experimental tools for continuing exploration of the past. We should utilize or discard such concepts according as they better explain what we already know, bring to light what we and our predecessors have ignored, or provoke a valuable realignment of the total picture we have of the past and of our fields of literary study. (I take it as beyond debate that we need concepts, and consequently their outward signs, or labels, in order to function at all.)

In this regard, it must be confessed that the current application of the concept of mannerism to literature is barely limping after the ideal just proposed.[14] To begin with, the word itself, far more than the word *baroque*, is a liability, since it has carried, and still carries, in its baggage a bewildering assortment of contradictory or ambiguous connotations. Even in sixteenth-century usage *maniera*, or style, had as wide and diverse a currency as the modern Italian *maniera* and the modern English *manner* have. The idioms and derivatives that scholars have hunted down, that is, *di maniera*, *manieroso*, *manierato*, and *manierismo*, often have an imprecision deriving from that early household usage.[15] But whereas for us the adjective *mannered* is wholly negative, the sixteenth century, as we know, could often use *maniera* and its derivatives approvingly. One finds both approving and disapproving applications of the term in Giorgio Vasari, who started the word on its art history journey by using it in preference to the established word for literary style, the Latin-derived *stile* (already found in Dante), presumably because its root meaning of "hand" seemed more applicable to works produced by the artist's hand. Needless to say, even in Vasari the "hand" of *maniera* is not merely that of a laboring craftsman, since the word is already for him a metaphor of the artist's skill and learning and mind.[16]

After Vasari's time, however, the term *mannerism*, like the term *baroque*, was used pejoratively by classicizing critics who wished to disparage post-High Renaissance art. In their hands it was a value term (that is, signifying mannered or bad style or lack of true style) rather than a neutral historical designation. Consequently, we are obliged to disregard all the negative connotations of our inherited word *mannered* when we deal with *mannerism*, despite the common root of the terms. This does *not* mean that we must avoid using our word *mannered* to characterize literary specimens of the so-called mannerist period, which we indeed find *mannered* in our negative sense. Even Shearman would agree, I think, that we are entitled to this privilege, provided of course we first make his recommended objective approach, putting aside any crude suspicions we may have that, when style itself becomes the goal of art, no good art can come of it.[17]

Further research into the terminology of mannerism seems fruitless. We know enough now about the early use and history of the terms. Our problem is to agree on the current meaning of the words *mannerism* and *mannerist* as applied to literature, reserving the right, *pace* Shearman, to distinguish good from bad mannerist works. That a work that is affected, pretentious, slavishly imitative, empty of meaning, a mere display of virtuosity, could be applauded in the sixteenth century does not mean we are bound to applaud it now. As literary historians and critics, we must take into account what such a work has to tell us about its time; we must give it every chance to speak its own language to us.

But we are not obliged either to love it or rate it above what we honestly consider to be its final worth for us.

At present, literary mannerism is being discussed in quite different ways, according to which theory has been accepted or is being tested by the literary critic venturing to fish in these murky waters. One approach, associated with Ernst Robert Curtius and continued in varying ways by such stylisticians as Gustav René Hocke, Helmut Hatzfeld, and Georg Weise, identifies literary mannerism with formal eccentricity, verbal ornamentation, and pointed thought.[18] For Curtius it is also a recurring phenomenon in the history of style. Since its prime language is rhetorical excess, and since it breaks out like a rash after, and even during, periods when ideal classical values are prized, it is evidence of a perennial human inclination to respond to order, symmetry, balance, clarity, and restraint (in sum, the so-called classical values) by reveling in excessive verbal artifice and complex meaning. Insofar as the Attic and Asiatic styles are both antique—to take an example from the history of prose style—and the rhetorical ornaments and verbal ambiguities also have their ancient pedigree, the mannerist writer in this sense may often claim to be classical, too. Victims of this disease are said to include François Rabelais and James Joyce as well as Marino and Góngora.

The studies of a Georg Weise, however, focus far less on these larger issues than on examples of Curtius's mannerist style in works of *the* mannerist period.[19] And in a study by Ulrich Schulz-Buschaus of that supposedly most mannerist of forms, *Das Madrigal,* the sixteenth-century "Manieristische Madrigal" is only one of the several types of madrigal discussed.[20] But here, too, the mannerist elements turn out to be the familiar tricks of punning and rhyming that Curtius first claimed as mannerist rather than baroque. Similarly Klaus-Peter Lange's monograph *Theoretiker des literarischen Manierismus* deals with, of all people, Emanuele Tesauro and Mateo Pellegrini, who were once Benedetto Croce's baroque theorists and later Joseph A. Mazzeo's theorists of the metaphysical style.[21]

The *Stilgeschichte* of Curtius and his followers has a fundamental attraction for the literary scholar befuddled by the problem of mannerism. It tells him that what he already knows is really what mannerism is all about, and it does not compel him to put up with the kind of juggling of paintings and poems or statues and plays that he will find gracing (and disgracing) other theories. Before turning to these other theories, it may be revelant to point out that the Curtius brand of literary mannerism is too self-contained in literary history to help solve our problem, which is to determine whether there is a relationship between the art and literature of a particular time that justifies the adoption of a common label implying a common set of esthetic values, as is the case with the terms *Renaissance* and *baroque.* There are two other practical reasons why we could not use Curtius's mannerism empty, as he would have it, of its art history content: For one, it would be awkward to have scholars working in the same general field employing the same word with two different meanings. Second, we do not need the term as he uses it since we have plenty of others, like *mannered, rhetorical,* and *witty,* which could be applied in a purely literary way when needed.

The second general theory of literary mannerism available does proceed from the other arts and seeks to embrace literature in its sweep. This theory, associated with the origins of the modern discussion of mannerism in German expressionism, defines the concept in terms of its alleged causes (religious, political, and sociological) and relies in its analyses on psychoanalytic theory, social history, the history of ideas, and other tools in the potting shed of modern critics. The key words here are *tension, anxiety, ambiguity, neurosis, strain, discord.*[22] As espoused in various ways by Hauser, Sypher, Artz, Roy Daniells, Daniel B. Rowland, and even Mary McCarthy, this *Angst* mannerism, as I like to call it, sees the formal and stylistic aberrations of post-High Renaissance literary art as legitimate and deep responses to the crises of the sixteenth century and, in some cases, truly amazing prophetic anticipations of the abstract art of the twentieth century. Its art heroes are Michelangelo, Pontormo, El Greco, and Parmigianino, in some instance Rosso and Tintoretto, in many instances Bronzino, and a nod in the direction of Daniele da Volterra, Giulio Romano, and Benvenuto Cellini. Its favorite literary exemplars are *Hamlet,* the work of the Jacobean playwrights, John Donne's *Anniversaries* and certain lyrics, *Don Quixote,* almost all of Torquato Tasso, and some of Marino along with Agrippa D'Aubigné and Luis de Góngora. In quantity and quality, the production of the proponents of *Angst* mannerism ranges from the massive two-volume survey by Hauser to Mary McCarthy's brief but hilarious comment on Pontormo's *Deposition* in *The Stones of Florence.*[23]

A third theory of literary mannerism, popularized by John Shearman but formulated earlier, pooh-poohs all the aforementioned emphasis on stress and strain and posits instead a healthy standard of elegant refinement. For Shearman, there is nothing neurotic or disturbing about mannerism. Historically, the painting of the *maniera* is not to be associated with the earlier aberrations of Rosso and Pontormo but with the later estheticism of Vasari's generation. Descriptively it is "the stylish style." A statue by Giambologna and Tasso's *Aminta* share an esthetic goal of being nothing other than their beautiful selves. Mannerism in literature, as in the other arts, is style, for style's sake, feeling perfectly secure in its classical pedigree and in its mission of advancing beyond the great cinquecento masters in ultimate refinement, without "a failure of nerve." [24] Mannered it will seem to us; beautiful it seemed to them and should seem to us. Shearman sees elements of his mannerism as early as the time of the court entertainer Serafino as well as in Ariosto and Giambattista Guarini. In fact, although he says he does not think mannerism was the *only* style possible in the sixteenth century, he well nigh characterizes most of its literature and culture as such. One comes away with the impression that the cinquecento is the Age of Mannerism.

Curiously enough, considering that Curtius will have no truck with art history, Shearman accepts and uses his purely literary definition of mannerism by drawing parallels, for example, between rhetorical figuration and the mannerist stylistic vocabulary. Thus, the *contrapposti* of the *figura serpentinata* are approximated to the verbal *contrapposti,* or antitheses, of Guarini's style in the *Pastor Fido* (hitherto regarded as hallmarks of the baroque style), presumably on the ground that they share a common esthetic goal of being delightfully "artificial" and that they are revelatory of their creators' facility in overcoming difficulty with *grazia.*[25]

The result of my review of these theories of literary mannerism must surely be that confusion predicted earlier. In one sense, everything is mannerist or possibly baroque. In another, equally disturbing, sense, only good works are mannerist, or only bad ones are. Is mannerism anticlassical, or is it the ultimate refinement of classicism? Silver rather than Golden Age? Is Tasso mannerist or baroque? Was Francesco de Sanctis wrong when he argued that Ariosto's virtue was precisely his lack of any *maniera?* What has John Lyly to do with John Donne? Did the French court fawn upon the upstart Philippe Desportes in preference to old Pierre de Ronsard because it was attuned to the new mannerism, or did it recognize that Ronsard was an incipient mannerist? Is Montaigne's rejection of the norms of Renaissance prose a mannerist gesture or baroque defiance? Is Cellini's blatant egotism a reflection of the new status of the artist as a creature of extraordinary *virtù* or a final flaunting of Renaissance individualism in the repressive atmosphere of post-Tridentine Italy?

In response to these questions and to the dilemma they pose for the concept of literary mannerism, I would suggest some general working principles and methods that may be helpful in future investigation.

First, I believe we may accept the hypothesis that there may be a literary style intervening between, and different enough from, its Renaissance prologue and its baroque epilogue to be worth studying. (Whether this style is part of an ever-recurring cycle in literary history or not, ought not to trouble us, since in any event we are concerned with its peculiar manifestation in the sixteenth and early seventeenth centuries.)

Second, we should not ignore, as Shearman, for one, largely does, the valuable insights into changes in the formal and representational ideals of the High Renaissance given us by the proponents of an *Angst* mannerism, even if we reject some of their explanations and characterizations as too obviously influenced by modern interests. There is, after all, a parallel between the ideals of Renaissance artists, with regard to the representation of space and the ideal proportions of the human figure, and the assumptions of Renaissance writers, with regard to the representation of human thought and action in the various literary genres and forms. If a development does occur in the other arts, then we ought also to look for it in literature, not simply in the rhetorical devices of poems, but in their total structures. One particularly useful method in this respect is to contrast the manner in which a succession of authors treat the same theme. Their response to this thematic challenge often reveals their poetic assumptions, their tastes, even, as the sixteenth century itself thought, their talent or lack of it. We will discover, if I may predict, much pure imitation with little or no real transformation of the basic material—what I would call *mannered* rather than mannerist. But we may also find, as in the case of a Marino or Scève imitating a Petrarchan theme, a different kind of formal presentation of the source, stressing different poetic values and therefore indicating a different underlying poetic. It may turn out that this different underlying poetic has some relationship to the other arts, and it may even have a common cause.[26]

Third, if we *must* speculate on causes as we go, before we reach critical conclusions, we should assume, as Boase suggests, that many motives are possible, simultaneously. John Donne may have written differently from the other Elizabethans, insofar as he did, for any number of reasons ranging from his personal *Angst* to his artist's sense that he had to surpass his great predecessors and talented contemporaries.

Fourth, we should think in terms of mannerist poems and plays, not mannerist authors. The same author, say Tasso or Marino or Góngora, or better Andrew Marvell, can write an old-fashioned Renaissance poem as well as a new-fangled mannerist or baroque one. An exemplary figure among minor poets of the English seventeenth century is Thomas Carew, that eclectic par excellence, who can sing "Give me more love, or more disdain:" as though it were still 1590, then put us through the metaphorical complexities of his "A Looking-Glasse," then invite us to squint at that "Mole in Celias Bosome." Note, too, the happy collocation in the Penguin Book of French Verse of Jean de Sponde's "Mais si faut-il mourir" and another sonnet beginning, "Si j'avais comme vous, mignardes colombelles," the latter being as private, meditative, elusive, even obscure as the former is public, hortotary, vivid, and painfully clear.[27] They are both sonnets, but they are different poems, in their structure, tone, imagery, and effect.

Fifth, we should look at literary works in their own terms and define our conclusions accordingly. In most instances, the features and qualities of mannerist art—representational, formal, stylistic—cannot be precisely identified in equivalent verbal structures. But having determined a distinct poetic, we may compare and contrast our findings with evidence from the other arts and possibly reach certain umbrella conclusions that would justify the judicious employment of a common label.

Sixth, we should distinguish between *mannered* and *mannerist,* letting the former term apply to such phenomena as mere imitation of classical sources or mere exaggeration of previous rhetorical manners.[28] Mannerism ought to be sought in those refinements, manipulations, distortions, and reshapings of Renaissance forms and ideals that achieve a distinct and individual poetic or esthetic profile—and let me note here my conviction that mannerist art is more individualistic than Renaissance art since it deviates subjectively from the norm, the public, and the expected, for better or worse. This approach would leave out most of cinquecento Petrarchism as merely mannered; it would exclude euphuism and Senecan tragedy as well; it would not assume that any genre or form is per se mannerist. The focus of this investigation would be on the prose of Montaigne, the manipulation of Renaissance narrative conventions by Cellini and Cervantes, Giordano Bruno's rejection of classical comic form in his comedy *Il Candelaio,* and the "wit" of the poetry of Tasso and Desportes and of some of the early lyrics of Marino. It would propose a new look at certain poems of Sidney, Raleigh, Herrick, and Marvell in addition to revisiting Donne and Thomas Carew. Since very little has been done with mannerist fiction and drama of our period, we should turn from analyzing the psychology of the heroes of such works to studying their formal modes of presentation—a troubled or dirty-minded or even psychotic hero does not make a work mannerist, but the way in which his story is told or his problem dramatized might well be revealing for our purposes.

I deliberately take up last a most vexing question of chronology, since my previous recommendations allow for a mannerism as early as Scève and as late as Marvell, thus overlapping with Renaissance and baroque. My acceptance of this eventuality is based on my earlier principle that we are dealing with a period in which several differing poetics were at times available simultaneously, and that literary artists of the time sometimes chose one, sometimes the other, for a variety of reasons. I know of no better explanation, for example, of why a Walter Raleigh should write his obscure "Ocean to Cynthia" quatrains and also his "Reply" to "The Passionate Sheepherd to his Love," or why a Góngora should abandon the early melodic clarity of his first manner in the lovely traditional Spanish forms for the murky, impenetrable style of his *Polifemo* and *Soledades.*[29] Obscure, impenetrable poetry (as opposed to the merely difficult) has, of course, a lineage dating from the *trobar clus* of the Troubadours, but even if we argue on strict historicist grounds that Renaissance obscurity (again, as opposed to the intellectual difficulty that was widely accepted and praised) was merely a revival of past obscure styles, we would have to explain why it was revived and regarded as an alternative in the later period. This speculation, however, should wait upon the preliminary achievement of a *total* phenomenology—not just a stylistic or thematic or rhetorical analysis—of the various literary works I have mentioned above. To use the terminology of that time, we should postpone our discussion of first and final causes until we have adequately grasped the material and formal ones.

One concluding caveat, too, on the *via negativa*, which I may appropriately voice now that the reader has my proposals for a positive and fruitful approach to the meaning of mannerism. Surely, there ought to be an end to any further comparisons of allegedly mannerist art and cognate literary works, with their loose, impressionistic renderings of supposedly similar "moods," "feelings," or even "ideas." Vague and irksome as they must inevitably be, these comparisons not only fog the subject of our concern but also "turn off" our colleagues, who become convinced that mannerism *is* meaningless, and that *all* attempts to bridge the arts are similarly doomed.[30]

I will conclude this paper with a summary that has emerged from my own struggles with the problem of mannerism, mindful of how sternly (and perhaps glibly, too) I have urged reason and care upon others. At present, I would venture the following general syncretic and tentative postulate about literary mannerism: mannerist art, on the whole, is parasitic and parodic in nature. It does seem to mark a break from the esthetic assumptions and the representational style of High Renaissance art, but, incongruously, it still depends upon that art for its effects upon the audience and for the evaluation of its creators. There would be no purpose in the complexity, the ambiguity, the unresolved or precariously balanced tensions and distortions of mannerist art, or in its equally startling refinements, were there not ever present a norm by which to judge its uniqueness, its differences from its predecessors and contemporaries, and its bravura skill. Whether or not its "unresolved tensions" reflect the anxieties of the age or the inability of the artists to solve esthetic problems they set for themselves, the overwhelming impression one has is that of a failure to be genuinely revolutionary in saying something new—Caravaggio's introduction of peasant types into sacred pictures seems to me more revolutionary than all of the mannerist distortions put together—and of a nearly total reliance on representational *means*. In mannerism the *mannered* is never far off because it is too easy to fall into mere quotation of one's predecessors, however exaggerated. At its best mannerist art seems capable of producing unquestioned masterpieces of its kind but, as the cliché would have it, few great works. Those few great works, nevertheless, do attest to the potential of the mannerist style when the freedom from norms it assumes takes precedence over the incongruous goal of rebellious imitation in the mind of a forceful artistic personality, the result being the masterpiece of a Michelangelo or a Tintoretto or an El Greco in that style. For literature, the same impulses toward deviation from the classical norms or from contemporary ideals based upon them could be satisfied by choosing and revitalizing alternatives from the tradition. Like the mannerist painter who teases humanist snobbery by deliberately evoking the hated Gothic manner (Vasari's *maniera gotica*), the poet of the time could pick as models, or create contemporary equivalents of, the works of those writers of late antiquity or the Middle Ages who created in a deviant style. For Renaissance writers seeking alternatives, the traditional codified esthetic imperative was *wit,* which in its literary sense means verbal or imagistic or formal complexity, distortion, compression, enlargement, enigma, obscurity, displacement—in sum, all of the deviations from the norm of clear, rational, coherent, and balanced presentation or structure. It is a truism, for example, that Spenser is not witty in this sense, nor is Ariosto (hence De Sanctis's feeling about his lack of a *maniera*), for neither poet draws attention to (or reveals) his formal "art," as "witty" writers always do, especially when they are being obscure or disjointed or shockingly "different." Thus, mannerist art in its literary manifestation is the art that reveals art.

Late Renaissance literature became more mannered than it had been all along and in some few instances became what we might call mannerist as it became more witty: witness the preference for compressed forms like the epigram and madrigal, for mixed genres, for non-Ciceronian prose, for satire and parody. (Nor did the baroque reverse this urge to wit; it continued to revel in the mannerist taste for the strange and the new but restored a harmony and coherence partly through reviving or continuing Renaissance ideals and partly through the imposition of framing and ordering philosophical and religious dogma.) Now in all of this, I contend, there is enough for a working hypothesis, or there is at least a basis for reexamining literary works of the time and their relationship to its art.

I am unsure whether or not it is a mannerist poem,[31] but there is a little verbal *jeu d'esprit* by Herrick, which I shall quote as my coda to these reflections on the pleasures and perils of the pursuit of a literary mannerism, of which it seems to me to be a singularly apt emblem:

> For sport my Julia threw a Lace
> Of silke and silver at my face;
> Watchet the silke was; and did make
> A shew, as if 't' ad been a snake:
> The suddenness did me affright;
> But though it scar'd, it did not bite.

> *Hesperides,* 1648 [32]

NOTES

JAMES V. MIROLLO is Professor of Comparative Literature, Columbia University. This paper is part of a comprehensive study of literary mannerism now in progress. Begun in the summer of 1968 with the aid of a grant from the American Council of Learned Societies, research into the problem was further facilitated by a Fulbright grant for study in Italy during 1968–69. The author expresses gratitude for help and inspiration to both these organizations, to his students at Columbia and New York University, and to several colleagues, especially Maurice J. Valency, Robert J. Clements, and Riccardo Scrivano.

1. Weisbach; "Der Manierismus," *Zeitschrift für Bildende Kunst* 30(1919), 161–83; Dvořák, "Greco und der Manierismus," *Wiener Jahrbuch für Kunstgeschichte* (1921), pp. 22–42. From the by-now vast art history literature on mannerism I shall be citing only those works that have importance for, or that include significant references to, the problem of literary mannerism, my main concern. It is obvious, however, that art historians like Weisbach, Dvořák, Heinrich Wölfflin, Walter Friedlaender, Erwin Panofsky, Ernst Gombrich, Giuliano Briganti, Anthony Blunt, Rudolf Wittkower, and their recent followers, whether in their occasional treatment of literary phenomena or in their wrestling with the concept of mannerism, have compelled those interested in a literary mannerism to take their work into account. Initially, the discussion of mannerism in the arts was faced with the task of putting aside inherited notions of stylistic aberration and frigid academicism, as well as Wölfflin's formulation of a merely "transitional" moment in the passage from Renaissance to baroque. Subsequently, such problems as the possibility of a perennial mannerism and the relationship of mannerism to baroque, to the Gothic, to the Counter-Reformation, to the so-called crisis of the late Renaissance, to classicism, to social transformations, and so on, have preoccupied most of the writers on the subject, with particular relevance, of course, for literature. In addition, such topics as the theory of imitation and the general esthetics and philosophical movements of the cinquecento also are vital, to say nothing of the larger questions of the chronology of mannerism within the periodization of the Renaissance itself. All this does not exclude, of course, as I indicate below, a particularly literary solution to the problem of mannerism.

2. Boase, "The Definition of Mannerism," *Proceedings of the Third Congress of the International Comparative Literature Association* (The Hague, 1962), pp. 43–55; Battisti, "Sfortune del manierismo," in *Rinascimento e Barocco* (Turin, 1960), pp. 216–57; Scrivano, "La discussione sul manierismo," *Cultura e letteratura nel Cinquecento* (Rome, 1966), pp. 231–84. Wellek's survey is now conveniently available in his *Concepts of Criticism* (New Haven, 1963). For Weise, see notes 18, 19 below.

3. It may be taken as axiomatic that paperback discussions of the subject, especially because of their availability to students and general readers, tend to become the definitive, if not the only, works known to such readers and to literary critics and historians who have an interest in mannerism but do not have the time or energy to keep up with their own fields and also delve into the huge bibliography on the subject. Thus, for example,

Wylie Sypher, Frederick Artz, Arnold Hauser, and John Shearman exerted an abnormal influence on the discussion of literary mannerism in the Donald J. McGinn and George Howerton anthology, which has a division entitled "Mannerism" (*Literature as a Fine Art* [Evanston, Illinois and New York, 1959] pp. 46–90); in such studies as Daniel B. Rowland, *Mannerism—Style and Mood* (New Haven, 1964), Roy Daniells, *Milton, Mannerism and Baroque* (Toronto, 1963), and Louis L. Martz, *The Wit of Love* (Notre Dame and London, 1969); and in such shorter commentary as Harold M. Priest's introduction to his anthology of *Renaissance and Baroque Lyrics* (Evanston, Ill., 1962) and Frank J. Warnke's essay "Metaphysical Poetry and the European Context," in *Metaphysical Poetry*, ed. Malcolm Bradbury and David Palmer (Bloomington, Ill., and London, 1971), pp. 260–76. European critics writing on literary mannerism tend to depart from a deep immersion in the bibliography of mannerism, though not necessarily with more satisfactory results: Riccardo Scrivano, *Il manierismo nella letteratura del Cinquecento* (Padua, 1959); and Marcel Raymond's introduction to his anthology *La Poésie française et le manièrisme* (Geneva, 1971). As regards the paperbacks, enormous influence has been exerted, as we shall see, by Ernst Robert Curtius's *European Literature and the Latin Middle Ages* tr. Willard R. Trask (New York, 1963), whose pages on mannerism are often preferred because they do without art history, and defiantly so (pp. 273–301).

4. Artz, *From the Renaissance to Romanticism: Trends in Style in Art, Literature, and Music, 1300–1830* (Chicago, 1963); Sypher, *Four Stages of Renaissance Style* (New York, 1955); Hauser, *The Social History of Art*, II (New York, 1957), and *Mannerism: The Crisis of the Renaissance and the Origin of Modern Art* (London, 1965); and Shearman, *Mannerism* (London, 1967). For the important studies of Georg Weise, see note 18 below.

5. (Princeton, 1970), pp. 40–54.

6. "La Définition du terme 'Baroque'," *Proceedings of the Third Congress of the International Comparative Literature Association* (The Hague, 1962), pp. 167–78.

7. For Martz and Warnke, see note 3 above. In *The Heirs of Donne and Jonson* (New York and London, 1970), Summers says in the preface, "For the seventeenth century . . . one can discover almost as many aesthetics as there are interesting poets," and later reaffirms his conviction of the inadequacy of the label *metaphysical* (pp. 13–16).

8. See, Antero Meozzi, *Il secentismo europeo* (Pisa, 1936), which sums up the previous development of this notion; and James V. Mirollo, *Poet of the Marvelous* (New York and London, 1963), which deals with the poet Marino's posthumous reputation, a key example of the application of a theory of European decadence now understood to be a reaction to mannerism and baroque (pp. 92–111). As we shall see, the idea of a Europe-wide decadence of style persists in contemporary discussion of mannerism.

9. Hiram Haydn, *The Counter-Renaissance* (New York, 1950). Eugenio Battisti does not emphasize "causes" but rather tries to depict a counter or underworld of the Renaissance in which the irrational, the fantastic, and the bizarre prevail (*L'antirinascimento* [Milan, 1962]). See also André Chastel, *The Crisis of the Renaissance, 1520–1600* (New York, 1968); and Baird W. Whitlock, "The Counter-Renaissance," *Bibliothèque d'humanisme et Renaissance*," 20(1958), 434–49.

10. On the concept of the Renaissance, the fundamental work is Wallace K. Ferguson, *The Renaissance in Historical Thought* (Boston, 1948). It may be supplemented by Denys

Hay, ed., *The Renaissance Debate* (New York, 1965); Tinsley Helton, ed., *The Renaissance: A Reconsideration of the Theories and Interpretations* (Madison, Wis., 1964); and Robert S. Lopez, *The Three Ages of the Italian Renaissance* (Charlottesville, Va., 1970). On the relationship of the periodization of the Renaissance to the discussion of mannerism, see Scrivano, *Il manierismo,* pp. 5–23.

11. Note, for example, the treatment of mannerism and baroque in Praz, *Mnemosyne;* of the baroque in Martz, *The Wit of Love,* and in Robert T. Petersson, *The Art of Ecstasy* (New York, 1970), to cite only a few recent studies in English. A large number of books and articles in many languages dealing with baroque literature and art could easily be added if space and the limits of our subject permitted. Certainly this phenomenon will be central in any updating of Wellek's survey.

12. *The Late Italian Renaissance, 1527–1633* (New York, 1970), in the Stratum Series of paperbacks dealing with historical problems.

13. The English literature textbook of McGinn and Howerton, *Literature as a Fine Art,* is the only one I know of that adopts the scheme Renaissance, mannerism, baroque, rococo. The usual practice is to avoid the terms completely or, in a few instances, to have references to, or brief discussions of, Continental styles or art phenomena that may bear some relationship to the English works included. In Europe, however, the baroque has gained wide acceptance, and the term *mannerism* is being increasingly used in academic centers.

14. There have been several large-scale attempts not yet cited in these notes: the journal *Esprit créateur,* 6(1966), devoted an entire issue to "French Manneristic Poetry between Ronsard and Malherbe," which included articles by Helmut A. Hatzfeld, Richard A. Sayce, and others. The Neuvième stage international d'études humanistes at Tours in 1965 also took up mannerism in relation to French poetry of the sixteenth century; its acts, published in *Lumières de la Pléiade* (Paris, 1966), included presentations by Marcel Raymond, Raymond Lèbegue, Victor L. Saulnier, Henri Weber, and other prominent critics.

15. On the word and the early usage, see Anthony Blunt, *Artistic Theory in Italy, 1450–1600* (Oxford, 1962), pp. 86–159; Mieczyslaw Brahmer, "Le 'manièrisme' terme d'histoire littéraire," *Acta Literaria Academicae Scientarum Hungaricae,* 5 (Budapest, 1962), 251–57; Giuliano Briganti, "Notizie sulla fortuna storica del manierismo," *Il manierismo e Pellegrino Tibaldi* (Rome, 1945), pp. 39–49; (Engl. tr. by Margaret Kunzle, Leipzig, 1962). Luigi Coletti, "Intorno alla storia del concetto di manierismo," *Convivium,* 16 (1948), 801–11; G. Nicco Fasola, "Storiografia del manierismo," *Scritti in onore di L. Venturi* (Rome, 1956), I, 429–47; Mario Treves, "*Maniera,* the History of a Word," *Marsyas,* 1(1941), 69–88; Georg Weise, "*Maniera* und *Pellegrino:* Zwei Lieblingswörter der italienischen Literatur der Zeit des Manierismus," *Romanistisches Jahrbuch,* 3(1950), 321–403; and "La Doppia origine del concetto di manierismo," in *Studi vasariani* (Florence, 1952), pp. 181–85. See also Georg Weise, "Le Manièrisme: Histoire d'une terme," *L'Information d'histoire de l'art,* 7(1962), 113–125; and "Storia del termine *manierismo,*" read at the symposium of the Academy of the Lincei in 1960 at Rome and published in *Manierismo, barocco, rococo* (Rome, 1962), pp. 27–38. From this important collection see also Ezio Raimondi, "Per la nozione di manierismo letterario," pp. 57–79.

16. On Vasari's use of the term, see John G. Freeman, ed., *The Maniera of Vasari,* tr. Mrs. Jonathan Foster (London, 1867); Walter Friedlaender, *Mannerism and Anti-Mannerism in Italian Painting,* (New York, 1957); Craig H. Smyth, *Mannerism and*

Maniera (New York, 1963); Marco Rosci, "Manierismo e accademismo nel pensiero critico del Cinquecento," *Acme*, 9(1956), 57–81. Scrivano has acutely pointed out that for Vasari *maniera* refers variously to the genius of the artist himself, his individual style, which may become a larger "school" or style through his followers, and in turn the *maniera*, or style, of an era in the epic history of art, in which he may be seen in retrospect as the characteristic force, for example, Giotto and Michelangelo (*Il manierismo*, pp. 44–45).

17. Shearman, *Mannerism*, pp. 15–22.

18. Hocke, *Manierismus in der Literatur* (Hamburg, 1959). A student of Curtius, Hocke indicates his interest in verbal and formal aberration by his subtitle, "Sprach-Alchimie und esoterische Kombinationskunst," and by his earlier volume, *Die Welt als Labyrinth: Manier und Manie in der europäische Kunst* (Hamburg, 1957). In his survey and in his anthology of German translations appended to *Manierismus in der Literatur*, Hocke ranges from Asiatic prose to such moderns as James Joyce, T. S. Eliot, and Arthur Rimbaud. Hatzfeld combines stylistic analysis and very controversial suggestions for classifying and periodizing European authors and styles in a series of essays, the most recent being "Literary Mannerism and Baroque in Spain and France," *Comparative Literature Studies*, 7(1970), 419–36; see also his "Italia, Spagna e Francia nello sviluppo della letteratura barocca," *Lettere italiane*, 9(1957), 1–29; his contribution to the *Esprit créateur* volume cited in note 14 above; and "The Baroque from the Viewpoint of the Literary Historian," *Journal of Aesthetics and Art Criticism*, 14(1955), 156–64. For Weise's contribution on the vogue for antithesis and oxymora in Italy, France, England, and Spain see "Manierismo e letteratura," *Rivista di letterature moderne e comparate*, 13(1960), 5–52; 19(1966), 253–78; 21(1968), 85–127.

19. Weise, fundamentally an art historian, departs from his long-argued belief that late Gothic survival combines with contemporary Renaissance to account for the art and the literary mannerist features of the period, regardless of whether or not there is also a perennial mannerism in all the arts. For a critique of Weise's approach emphasizing the limits of *Stilgeschichte*, and also discussing his earlier books and articles dealing with Renaissance and mannerism in Italian art and literature of the fifteenth and sixteenth centuries see Riccardo Scrivano, "Gli studi di Georg Weise sul Rinascimento e sul manierismo," *Cultura e letteratura nel Cinquecento*, pp. 267–313. Praz asserts, however, that Weise's oxymora and antitheses are stock phrases and commonplaces rather than structural characteristics (*Mnemosyne*, p. 226, n. 40). One gathers that Praz, stressing "tension and counterpoint" as the main qualities of mannerism and dissatisfied with the formulations of Weise and Shearman, adheres in the main to the interpretations of *Angst* mannerism, especially Hauser's.

20. As indicated in advance by the subtitle, "Zur Stilgeschichte der italienischen Lyrik zwischen Renaissance und Barock" ([Bad Homburg, 1969], esp. pp. 80–101).

21. (Munich, 1968); Mazzeo, *Renaissance and Seventeenth-Century Studies* (New York, 1964), pp. 29–59; Croce's pioneering study of the Italian treatises and that of Baltasar Gracian appeared in *Problemi di estetica* (Bari, 1934), pp. 311–48.

22. These terms, plus others like *alienation* (Hauser's key term), *doubt*, and *torment*, may be found on every page of the critics mentioned, but especially in Sypher, who has perhaps been excessively maligned for this practice as well as his habit of mismatching literary

and art works on the basis of such terminology; like Shearman, Sypher has become the symbol, for many, of an extreme position on mannerism, clouding the valuable insights he contributes in developing that position. Undoubtedly, both Sypher and Shearman were hampered by the need to reach a general readership, but one may ask, especially in the case of Shearman, whether the format involved was the proper place to present a partial view.

23. (New York, 1959), pp. 108–14.

24. The phrase is used by Kenneth Clark for the title of his Bickley Lecture printed in *A Failure of Nerve: Italian Painting 1520–1535* (Oxford, 1967). However, it was used earlier in the more negative sense I intend by Eugenio Battisti; he asserts that the trouble with mannerism generally is its "mancanza di coraggio" (*Rinascimento e barocco* [Turin, 1960], p. 225).

25. *Mannerism*, pp. 91–96; Praz also makes much of the *linea serpentinata* as the common formula of mannerism, finding its literary equivalent in the poetry ("torturous reasoning") of Donne and the *"serpentinata* prose" of Sidney, while agreeing with Weise in generally excluding Euphuism from mannerism (*Mnemosyne*, pp. 90–101); Martz also refers several times to Donne's "movement" as "unstable, constantly shifting" and to his "manner" as "curiously shifting and winding toward truth" (*The Wit of Love*, pp. 34–39). Praz here recapitulates his earlier discussions of Sidney and Donne (*Ricerche angla-italiane* [Rome, 1944], pp. 63–78; "Baroque in England," *Modern Philology*, 61(1964), 169–79.

26. One must look for an underlying poetic because there does not seem to be in any literary criticism of the time a formal and coherent statement of such a poetic, although one finds in Lodovico Castelvetro, in Girolamo Fracastoro, in Sperone Speroni, and others occasional opposition to certain classical or standard Renaissance ideas about imitation, the nature and purposes of poetry, and the regular genres. It is well known that in England no supporting contemporary theory exists for "metaphysical" poetry except for poetic appreciations like Thomas Carew's of Donne's style; Italian and French theorizing is largely Horatian-Aristotelian, with some deference to proponents of Plato and, especially in Spain, to the exigencies of the Counter-Reformation. (The seventeenth-century theorists of wit in Italy and Spain I take to be philosophizers and codifiers of the baroque poetic already in vogue and already having absorbed some mannerist features.) Attention to this sixteenth-century theorizing by Bernard Weinberg and Baxter Hathaway, following upon the older studies of Joel Spingarn and Ciro Trabalza, has not revealed either a mannerist or pre-baroque theory. Nor does the Ariosto-versus-Tasso debate, the defense of Dante, or the question of the language produce in Italy a coherent or systematic theory that might be called the theory of mannerist poetry. Blunt and other art historians, on the other hand, point to late cinquecento treatises for a cluster of ideas (Platonic idealism, the *disegno interno*, *grazia*, nonimitation of nature, and the emphasis on *maniera*) capable of being interpreted as an esthetics of mannerism; but there is no real literary equivalent, despite the known literary sources of these art treatises.

27. (Baltimore, 1964), pp. 154–55, 160; Raymond excludes both poems from his anthology of French mannerist poetry but includes several others. It is well known that Sponde, like Marino, was once discussed and treated exclusively as either metaphysical or baroque.

28. Hatzfeld defines mannerism in terms of a "trend whereby, from the sixteenth century onward, the clever Renaissance styles of Petrarch and Ariosto faded away into a multi-

plicity of *maniere*" and goes on to analyze instances in Boscán, Garcilaso, and Ronsard, which I would characterize as either mannered or effective manipulations of sources ("Literary Mannerism and Baroque," pp. 420ff.). Hatzfeld also includes Euphuism, Marinism, and gongorism among his *maniere*.

29. The editor of Raleigh, Agnes Latham, says of "Cynthia": "To come to *Cynthia* desiring logic, form and coherence is to be disappointed. . . . It represents Ralegh in his obscurest mood. . . . the reader must be content with a beautiful confusion" (*The Poems of Sir Walter Raleigh* [Cambridge, 1962], pp. xxxi–xxxii). It is interesting to note, from my point of view, the editor's assumption that, since the work is a "fragment," its difficulties might be solved if we had the whole, revealing a reluctance to accept the possibility of an obscure work per se (*ibid.*, p. xxxii).

30. Equally to be eschewed is the frequent and glib reference to a work as "undoubtedly mannerist," or to a poetic form or a whole genre as such, whether it is the madrigal or the tragicomedy or the pastoral romance. Undoubtedly, the vogue or taste for a particular poetic form or genre at any time is an index of a new or different underlying poetic, but that poetic may be fruitfully explored only in the style of individual works considered as such.

31. Praz would consider it in relationship to the baroque because of Herrick's interest in the silks of women's dresses and his emphasis upon "significant movement" rather than a beautiful stillness (*Mnemosyne*, pp. 121–25). Others might point to the habit of mannerist painters of focusing on accessory features or depicting shot silk, to the terseness and ambiguity of the content, or even to the compact form in order to claim it as mannerist. In opposition, there would be those who would argue that a poet like Herrick, insulated as he supposedly was from Continental art and literature of his day, dependent upon his reading of classical authors and contemporary English poets, could hardly be involved with mannerism, no less.

32. *The Complete Poetry of Robert Herrick*, ed. J. Max Patrick (New York, 1963), pp. 158–59. I should add in this final note several other references to works relevant to our discussion but not yet cited: Mario Praz, "Milton e Poussin," *Gusto neoclassicismo* (Naples, 1959), pp. 1–38; Jerome Mazzaro, *Transformations in the Renaissance English Lyric* (Ithaca, N.Y., 1970); Mario Richter, "Philippe du Plessis-Mornay: Un aspetto del 'manierismo' poetico protestante," *Contributi dell' Istituto di Filologia Moderna dell' Universita Cattolica*, 3(1964), 1–20; Kurt Reichenberger, "Der literarische Manierismus des ausgebenden 16. und beginnenden 17. Jahrhunderts in Frankreich," *Romanistisches Jahrbuch*, 13(1962), 76–86; Ferruccio Ulivi, *Il manierismo del Tasso e altri studi* (Florence, 1966); Hugo Friederich, *Epochen der italienischen Lyrik*, (Munich, 1964); Enrico Carrara, "Il manierismo letterario di Benvenuto Cellini," *Studi romanzi*, 19(1928), 171–200; R. O. Jones, "Renaissance Butterfly, Mannerist Flea: Tradition and Change in Renaissance Poetry," *Modern Language Notes*, 80(1965), 166–84; Dámaso Alonso, y Carlos Bousoño, *Seis Calas en la expressión literaria española* (Madrid, 1963), and esp. "Poesía correlativa inglesa en los siglos XVI y XVII," pp. 327–77; Rosemond Trive, "Baroque and Mannerist Milton," *Milton Studies in Honor of Harris Francis Fletcher* (Urbana, Ill., 1961), pp. 209–25; Elbert B. O. Borgerhoff, "Mannerism and Baroque: A Simple Plea," *Comparative Literature*, 5(1953), 323–31, the ignoring of whose simple plea has influenced the hazarding of the complex plea above.

2

IMAGE AND CONSCIOUSNESS
IN SCÈVE'S *DÉLIE*

Thomas M. Greene

COMMUNICATION across the humane disciplines is useful when, as in the present case, it invites us to measure and define our respective intuitions of a common historical concept. My remarks will aim chiefly at isolating certain elements which, it seems to me, could properly be considered mannerist in a work to which that term has frequently been applied. But I'd like to preface the discussion of Maurice Scève by sketching my view of the kind of usefulness a term such as *mannerism* offers to the literary scholar. Perhaps the pursuit of a mannerist literature is itself a mannerist enterprise—given to nervous self-questioning, abstraction, tension, and instability. The term first made its way among students of literature as a foster child whose presence in our midst was a little suspect, and whose legitimacy could be proved only by reasserting a sacred marriage between literature and the visual arts. In this early stage of our education, we discovered mannerism *analogically*, by reference to patterns of painting or sculpting or building whose structures we could make out to resemble, by a kind of metaphoric transfer, the verbal structures we wanted to understand. It seems to me that this stage, associated with such scholars as Wylie Sypher and Roy Daniells, is now behind us; [1] that if the concept of mannerism is to find a permanent literary shelter, it must be accorded its own integrity and independence as a properly *literary* tool, whatever clouds of visual associations it continues to trail. The day is past, or should be past, when the allegedly mannerist character of *Lycidas* needs to be defended by reference to the Medici chapel. As early as 1948 Ernst Robert Curtius was discussing a mannerism based purely on verbal devices, and some European scholars are beginning to follow his example. [2] To imitate them, we must be free from the embarrassing suspicion of pushing a metaphor too hard; we must not, to be sure, close our eyes to its ulterior usage, but we must welcome the accretion of specifically literary meaning to a suggestive critical tool.

Suggestive, indeed, is the apt word, and I for one would be sorry to see this concept become either more or less than that. I share the hope of W. K. Wimsatt, Jr., that a term like *mannerism* "will never clarify or harden into any kind of determinate or literal validity for literary criticism." [3] One danger of pressing the analogy with the visual arts would be to insist on a mannerist age in European poetry as valid as the age of, say, mannerist architecture. It may be that literary styles cross national boundaries less tidily than architectural styles, faced as they are with higher linguistic barriers. It may be that literary history is inherently still messier than art history, and that our own historical categories must leave room for lines of development still more disheveled, asymmetrical, confused, and diffused than those in the other arts. A concept like mannerism is illuminating to the degree that it helps to separate out certain lines of development rather than to scramble them together into a single period block. Claudio Guillén has recently pleaded for a literary history organized primarily by currents rather than by periods, a history capable of tracing the complex flow of modes and traditions as they run together and fork apart, swirl, reverse themselves, eddy, spend themselves, get lost in larger currents.[4] *Mannerism* is the sort of term that helps us follow one current, a very forceful one, in late Renaissance literature.

Within such a current it frequently occurs that a single author, or even a single work, realizes and intensifies and so to speak authenticates the diffused tendencies of its past tradition. Maurice Scève's *Délie* plays such a role in the history of the Petrarchan love convention, and especially that branch of it which depended upon precious ingenuity. The *Délie,* a sequence of 449 dizains, published with *imprese* at Lyon in 1544, pays homage to Petrarch himself, reflects the influence of the fashionable neo-Platonic philosophy of love, and occasionally recalls the third-rate wit of the Italian *strambottisti,* who flourished briefly before and after the turn of the sixteenth century. But the *Délie* brings to its tradition a concentration and a logic which it had seldom enjoyed; one way to understand the mannerist current that produced it is to examine this brilliant culmination of its earlier stages.

If one wanted to pursue the study of mannerist literature by analogy with the visual arts—as I do not—the career of Maurice Scève would provide a useful instance. For Scève, with Ronsard, was one of the few important poets of the Renaissance who designed a complex work joining poetry with the visual and performing arts. The medium of this work is the *Entrée,* the royal entry, a medium just beginning to reach its apogee when, in 1548, Scève superintended the preparations for the entry of Henri II into Lyon. André Chastel and Marcel Raymond have pointed out that the *Entrée* as an art form is itself quintessentially mannerist, with its ambiguous mingling of real and artificial, its transformation of the familiar into the imaginary, its disproportionate praise for the royal visitor, its ostentatious and scandalous opulence. The arches and sculptures executed under Scève's direction for the entry of Henri would appear to have been particularly representative of the mannerist style, in their obtrusive ornamentation, their *horror vacui,* and their intellectualized symbolism. The relation of Scève's poetic imagination to those works, which he describes in a little booklet commemorating the occasion, is a subject I leave to heads better equipped than mine to explore.[5] It seems to me in any case more promising, at the present stage of our understanding, to try to work out a mannerist poetic. As a step toward that goal, my remarks on the *Délie* here aim at analyzing a few elements which acquire in that work a peculiar resonance and which in my view are properly mannerist.

We may begin with a rhetorical figure, which is very common in *Délie* and which has been labeled mannerist first by Ernst Robert Curtius and again by Helmut A. Hatzfeld.[6] This is the figure which Quintilian called *periphrasis* or *circuitus eloquendi* and which we call periphrase or circumlocution. It might be defined as a figure that replaces the ordinary, simple, obvious word or phrase with a longer, less common, and less obvious expression. It underlies innumerable majestic and difficult passages in Dante's *Commedia*—I say "innumerable" because Curtius's figure of 150 seems to me conservative—and by the eighteenth century it issues in such swollen monstrosities as the allusion to an egg by an English poetaster as "the feathered cackler's pearly fruit." Pushed far enough it becomes a kenning or a riddle, and Hatzfeld quotes a running series of what he calls "riddle-circumlocutions" from another "mannerist" poet, Du Bartas. Scève's *Délie* is full of them, some riddling and some not, fuller doubtless than most earlier Petrarchan sequences, though he was by no means the first to introduce this figure into the convention. He refers to the sun as "the faithful adulterer of the ocean":

De l'Occean l'Adultaire obstiné [7] (11)

Or he indicates the arrival of spring by an astrological formula:

Phebus doroit les cornes du Thoreau (223)

Or he addresses Mount Fourvière, which overlooks his native city of Lyon and her rivers, as:

Mont costoyant le Fleuve, & la Cité . . . (412)

Or he signals the passage of two months:

Ja deux Croissantz la Lune m'à monstré (35)

Some of Scève's periphrases are metaphors, like the sun-adulterer, and others are not, like the address to Mount Fourvière, but it seems fair to say that when metaphor and periphrase coincide, we *hear* the expression primarily as periphrase, which thus becomes the dominant figure and the most vivid in our verbal consciousness. This effect may be due to the very weight and amplitude a periphrase necessarily entails. We are, at any rate, conscious of this figure repeatedly throughout *Délie,* and its presence contributes to that impression of highly wrought, artificial, and precious elegance which Scève's external world assumes.

But, let us note, *only* the external world. Periphrase is applied almost exclusively to objects and events outside the poet's own consciousness: occasionally to the lady, Délie, but most frequently and characteristically to the great natural forces and transformations that animate the natural cosmos—sun and moon, dawn and dusk, river and hill, month and season. The *Délie* indeed is a great hymn to the flow of nature: the flow of the Rhône and Saône rivers, and of hours and days, the changes from light to dark and dark to light, from summer fertility to winter ice and back again to spring rain, changes that sometimes imitate and sometimes violate the phases of the poet's heart. That outer realm of beautiful process is formalized, dignified, and stabilized by its periphrastic evocation.

Scève's periphrases *formalize* the outer world by investing it with an almost heraldic stiffness, a ceremonial majesty, withdrawing it from the commonplace and quotidian, until it becomes almost as artificial as the language that evokes it. When, referring to nightfall, he writes:

> . . . quand Vesper sur terre universelle
> Estendre vient son voile tenebreux . . . (355)

that formulation informs the common occurrence with a grave solemnity which reduces its natural character. This formalizing distortion of the natural world is in itself a mannerist effect. The formality is bound up with the *dignifying* function of periphrase, since it is used almost exclusively for those things the poet chooses to praise. The glossy and sinuous elegance seems to caress its subject. Mythology, so protean an instrument in the poetry of the Renaissance, serves here to distance and to magnify, to convey an honorific distinction apprehensible by a cultivated elite. Even when Scève refers to one of the most barbarous myths, the story of Procne and Philomela, he finds a periphrase so cool, so exquisitely precious, that the blood is forgotten. He writes:

> Les tristes soeurs plaignaient l'antique offense . . . (31)

This indeed is a double if not triple periphrase. "The mournful sisters were complaining of the ancient wrong" means that Procne and Philomela were complaining of Tereus's brutality, which means in turn that the swallow and nightingale were singing. This means, finally, by a familiar convention, that the hour was a spring evening. Scève's formula situates two referents, the evening and the rape, at opposite ends of a series of inferences required of the reader and in the process invests both referents with a certain artificial grace.

But, as this example shows, periphrase not only formalizes and dignifies; it also works a third effect, more difficult to isolate, which I have described as *stabilizing*. Although the periphrases in *Délie* often evoke the processes and changes of nature, their consequence, I submit, is to assert majestic natural permanence. If Vesper draws his shadowy veil over the universal earth, that is a detached and knowable event, but the event leads to a respect for the enduring, ineluctable, but never monotonous, continuities of the visible universe. If the mournful sisters complain on a particular spring evening, the very fact that the periphrase communicates establishes a world wherein nightingale and swallow sing every spring, a world of distinct, repetitive, and orderly phenomena. Although the periphrase tends to stress a single aspect of things and events, we feel it in *Délie* as an expression of achieved permanence; even when it is riddling or precious, its ultimate effect is reassuring.

This sense of permanence is all the more notable because we grasp the world in *Délie* only through a human consciousness that is itself unstable and fragmented. Indeed the reader is never permitted an escape from the troubled intensity of the speaker's inner self, and we glimpse the external world only as it impinges on him, only as it sets in motion his own restless mind. Scève assimilated his master Petrarch most faithfully, most profoundly, not in the accidents of imagery or rhetoric, but in this unrelieved interiority of the lover's consciousness. The voice we hear in the *Canzoniere* as in *Délie* issues from an imprisoned and narcissistic self, sealed in with a lonely intensity and perpetually in quest of equilibrium. In this respect, as well as in others, Petrarch may be regarded as a proto-mannerist. His isolation, like that of *Délie's* lover, is obsessive, frozen, strained, and out of balance.

To carry that sense of unstable fragmentation, a different rhetoric has to be made to work. The periphrase, conferring artifice, dignity, and permanence, is almost never applied to the poet's inner moods, transitory and divided as they are. Instead we are given paradoxes, answering to the psyche's shifting antitheses, and we are given metaphors, ingenious, forced, and yet frequently hazy, and when the metaphor is extended long enough to remind us of a periphrase, we miss any sense of periphrastic stability. The paradoxes dramatize that sense of inner tumult, of conflict and confusion amounting almost to collapse, which the poems repeatedly evoke. Some paradoxes are merely banal and trivial, superficial oxymorons echoing played out stereotypes. But other paradoxes lead to the poetic and dramatic core of the sequence and point to mysterious complexities that do not yield easily to rational explication:

. . . Sa lumiere est tousjours en tenebres. (330)

. . . presque mort, sa Deité m'esveille
En la clarté de mes desirs funebres. (7)

Lines like these evoke a twilight realm of inner process whose contradictory workings the reader may never hope fully to circumscribe. A single phrase in the liminal verse defines the subject of the sequence: "les mortz, qu'en moy tu renovelles." That concentrated phrase—"to renew deaths in me"—suggests at once two concurrent and opposite processes. The lady repeatedly brings the poet to the point of death, renews his suffering, but also repeatedly restores him, renews his life. The meanings of this one verb chase each other around a circle that resembles the circular workings of the poet's feeling. Paradox is at the center of his experience, but a paradox felt to be ambiguous and inconclusive. Rosalie Colie may speak truly for much Renaissance usage when she writes that "in paradox form and content, subject and object are collapsed into one, in an ultimate insistence upon the unity of being." [8] But the mannerist logic of *Délie* rather associates paradox with a conflict of being; it represents the simultaneously beneficial and destructive experience of love.

The metaphors that evoke the poet's inner consciousness participate in this impression of unstable contradiction. The metaphors of the *Délie* tend to be strained, jagged, and unexpected analogies, which impose themselves rudely on the delicate tissue of its discourse. Jealousy is a cricket; hope is a loadstone of calamities; pain is an alembic; fidelity is an emery on which to polish faith. In this context, metaphors like these are assimilated to the paradoxical rhetoric around them; they are themselves felt as paradoxical, as incomplete, as violating logic and order. They seem to force the mind toward a precarious equation which can only be seized briefly and tortuously. If the periphrase calls up an outer realm of stable continuities, the metaphor flashes up intermittently from an uncompleted inner realm of painful flux, frustration, and half-articulated mystery. Our impression of each realm depends not only on what we are told about it but also on the rhetoric that transmits the information.

The most elaborate periphrases tend to appear at the opening of the dizain, the most jarring conceits at the end. Whether or not these appear in a single poem, there is a characteristic movement from outer to inner landscape. This is the movement in dizain 98:

> Le Dieu Imberbe au giron de Thetys
> Nous fait des montz les grands umbres descendre:
> Moutons cornuz, Vaches, & Veaulx petitz,
> En leurs parcz clos serrez se viennent rendre.
> 　　Lors tout vivant a son repos veult tendre,
> Ou dessus moy noveau resveil s'espreuve.
> 　　Car moy constraint, & par forcée preuve
> Le soir me couche esveillé hors de moy,
> Et le matin veillant aussi me treuve,
> Tout esploré en mon piteux esmoy.

In this dizain, as in so many, the poet is out of phase with a natural universe that he leads us to see as harmonious. The spontaneous return of flocks to their enclosing and protective dwellings at nightfall imitates the return of the youthful Apollo, "le Deiu Imberbe," to the protective bosom of the sea-goddess Thetis. The second line echoes almost certainly the majestic close of Vergil's first Eclogue, wherein the exiled Meliboeus is urged by his fellow-shepherd Tityrus to delay his departure till morning, since nightfall is imminent, the village roofs are smoking in the distance, and shadows are lengthening from the mountain crests.

> . . . Iam summa procul villarum culmina fumant,
> Maioresque cadunt altis de montibus umbrae.

Scève's dizain follows Vergil in associating the mountains' lengthening shadows with hospitable repose and by setting against this repose the harshness of reluctant exile. But Scève's exile is of course subjective, and moreover it is dual. If, in his own private disorder, he is forcibly excluded from the grand natural rhythms of activity and repose, he is also, in a bolder and darker figure, "hors de moy," outside of *himself*—beside himself, we would say—but the cliché here finds a renewed force from its context. The poet is excluded even from the bonds of generation, delicately suggested by the juxtaposition in the third line of *Vaches* and *Veaulx petitz*. Like many love poems, this one is about more than love— about loneliness, exile, and the privacy of sorrow.

It moves, typically, from the universal, harmonious, the denaturalized and formalized order without, rendered periphrastically, to the particular, shifting, and unresolved turmoil within. One way to catch the implications of this movement is to consider the present tense of the successive verbs. The durative present of the first four lines—"fait," "se viennent"—narrates a specific, detached event happening now, and we follow it with the poet as it takes place before his eyes. But in the close, which describes the poet's retiring and waking, the present tense—"me couche," "me treuve"—opens out to embrace an indefinite past and future; it is no longer narrating an event but evoking a continuous, apparently unending series of reluctant rituals.

This use of the iterative present tense for a repeated, involuntary process within the poetic consciousness is extremely common in *Délie;* it really represents the basic phenomenology of the inner self. The objects and events without impinge upon the self, as in dizain 98, on separable occasions, but their consequences are typically caught up in a habitual and endless train.

Je cours soubdain, ou mes tourmentz m'appellent. (274)

Plus je la voy, plus j'adore sa face. (307)

Je cele en toy ce, qu'en moy je descouvre. (366)

Time becomes a treadmill or a trap, and the lover can only register wryly his helpless passivity. The orderly, sequential flow of the natural universe gives way to the weary, undifferentiated impulses of romantic habit. A similar effect is produced by Scève's characteristic way of substantivizing the infinitive form of the verb:

Ce mien languir multiplie la peine . . . (248)

    . . . le trop esperer
M'esmeult souvent le vacciler du doubte. (362)

a process which freezes the repeated movement of consciousness into a fixed attribute. This sense of time—for which Scève found many Petrarchan precedents, but which he renders more acute and more expressive—this sense of time as continuously constricting seems to me in itself essentially mannerist.

We might then regard dizain 98 as a mannerist poem in several respects: in the formal artifice and rhetorical distance of the opening periphrase, contrasting sharply with the warmth and visual immediacy of the image that follows; in the creative, but somewhat wrenched, adaptation of a Vergilian source; in the sense of impotent passivity conveyed by the closing lines; in the discrete barrier between external and internal process; and in the deterioration of an orderly, natural life-rhythm into a constricted, indefinite, painful one.

This constricted, iterative rhythm emerges with special force from the *imprese* that recur in *Délie* after every ninth dizain. Since the sixteenth century, these have been called emblems, and I shall follow the convention. The emblems are pictures containing a brief unrhymed motto set within a decorative surround; the motto is echoed by the last line of the following dizain. Most of the pictures themselves have nothing to do with love, and it requires a certain ingenuity to apply their mottoes to the poet's situation. Thus the fourth emblem portrays a man trying unsuccessfully to restrain an ox with a rope. The motto reads, "Plus l'attire plus m'entraine." The last line of the following dizain, referring to the lady, reads, "Plus je l'attire et plus a soy m'entraine." A certain amount of scholarly study has been brought to the history of these emblems, but nobody, I think, has asked what dramatic coloring they throw as a body upon the poetry. This is all the more surprising because in fact certain types of situations do tend to recur within the emblem pictures. Like the example I just cited, the emblems incline to situations where enterprise is self-defeating and fate plays cruel jokes. Other examples: a dying unicorn whose head rests on a woman's lap, with the motto "Pour la veoir je pers la vie"; two birds trapped in bushes coated with lime, and the motto "Ou moins crains plus suis pris"; a deer wounded by an arrow, pursued to a peak from which it cannot escape, and the motto "Fuyant ma mort j'haste ma fin." Not all the emblems fit this pattern equally well, but their cumulative force suggests a Kafkaesque bafflement of the will and a perpetual cruelty toward a misled victim. The motto is invariably phrased in that iterative present we have already traced through the dizains themselves. As in the poetry, the continuous present is associated with entrapment; the dying unicorn, the birds caught in lime, the fleeing deer are trapped like the donkey turning a millstone, whose motto is "Fuyant peine travail me suyt." By their ingenious cruelty and their peculiar rhetoric, the emblems serve to focus this aspect of Scève's mannerist phenomenology.

But Scève also leaves room, as we have seen, for single, particular events, just as he leaves room for a sudden blossoming of joy to punctuate his pain. *Délie* may be read as a struggle between the single detachable event—detachable even if like nightfall it forms part of a series—and the process of monotonous iteration. Dizain 98 is an example of the way an event gets lost in, or is swallowed up by, the iteration; there time seems to offer an opening into the specific, only to fall back on the closed circle of repetition. That pattern is common in Scève, but occasionally, as in dizain 79, the event beats off the challenge of recurrence and saves its own uniqueness:

L'Aulbe estaingnoit Estoilles a foison,
Tirant le jour des regions infimes,
Quand Apollo montant sur l'Orison
Des monz cornuz doroit les haultes cymes.
Lors du profond des tenebreux Abysmes,
Ou mon penser par ses fascheux ennuyz
Me fait souvent percer les longues nuictz,
Je revoquay a moy l'ame ravie:
Qui, dessechant mes larmoyantz conduictz,
Me feit cler veoir le Soleil de ma vie.

Here, as in dizain 98, the outer landscape presents a momentary image of grandiose beauty, expressed with periphrastic elaboration, from which we move inward, in line 5, to the precipitous landscape of the poet's consciousness, and then in lines 6 and 7, with the appearance of the significant adverb *souvent*, to a constrained rhythm of restlessness ("mon penser . . . Me fait souvent percer les longues nuictz"). The metaphoric "tenebreux Abysmes," associated with that restlessness, comprise a familiar motif which reappears many times in the *Délie* and which seems to denote a kind of psychic dissolution, a gulf of confusion and despair amounting almost to nonbeing. The poet's soul has been "ravie" —abducted, carried off to the depth of the abyss—as we gather it is repeatedly abducted. But on this occasion, he asserts his rational will and recalls the soul from the abyss to his awakening consciousness, as though inspired now by the dawning light itself, which in line 2 draws the day from the depths of chaos.

Thus this dizain chronicles a humanist victory. The shadow is dispelled, the gulf surmounted, and restless iteration yields in line 8 to the triumphant past definite "revoquay," which reasserts the particularity of the moment as it reasserts lucid control.

That victory is won through a vision of the lady in line 10, the Sun which dissipates shadows and dries tears. Between the opposing realms of the poem Délie moves with imperceptible grace. She alone belongs to both. The subtitle —"objet de plus haulte vertu"—seems to assert her objectivity, but the word *vertu* suggests an object of talismanic subjective power. The *vertu* of Délie is a power within the poet's mind, and if she remains a presence and a reality without, her reality can only reach him—and us—through the filter of his consciousness. He tells us this again and again, in so many words:

> Je le conçoy en mon entendement
> Plus, que par l'oeil comprendre je ne puis
> Le parfaict d'elle. (226)

And elsewhere:

> Je quiers en toy ce, qu'en moy j'ai plus cher. (271)

Délie's role is thus uniquely ambiguous, participating both in that constant formality of permanence beyond his reach and in the flux of his spirit. Thus we should expect her denomination to fall somewhere between periphrase and metaphor or to occupy their overlapping ground. This is in fact what commonly occurs. Should we regard the expression "le Soleil de ma vie" in dizain 79 as a timid periphrase or an unadventurous metaphor? Perhaps it is both. The same indeterminate and frequently traditional rhetoric governs most of the references to her; she is "cest Ange en forme humaine" or "mon Phoenix" or "mon Basilisque." A little surpisingly, the hundreds of references to Délie tend to lack the strong color and emphasis of Scève's other images, just as the woman herself, as we know her, lacks particularity. She appears to us, elusively and celestially regular, with all the pallor of her metaphysical ambiguity.

Only at those rare moments of the sequence when the conflict ends between events and iteration, objective and subjective, does the lady acquire full rhetorical force. At those moments the temporal conflict is resolved by a triumphant future tense, the outer and inner realms come together, and the metaphor achieves an unwonted stasis.

> Mais toy, qui as (toy seule) le possible
> De donner heur a ma fatalité,
> Tu me seras la Myrrhe incorruptible
> Contre les vers de ma mortalité. (378)

These famous lines depend on a metaphor that is brilliantly original but that we feel as stable and complete. So it is, again, with the metaphor that ends the entire sequence:

Nostre Genevre ainsi doncques vivra
Non offensé d'aulcun mortal Letharge. (449)

"Nostre Genevre," the juniper that *will* live, symbolizes eternity and unites lover and beloved in enduring equilibrium. In a few instances like these, the dialectic of *Délie* is transcended and its two poles meet.

Each of the poles is essentially mannerist—both the static, hieratic, periphrastic world of nature and the fluctuating, paradoxical, metaphoric world of the self. Moreover, it is typical of mannerist art in all mediums that it invites us to notice its rhetoric. Mannerist poets write as though to undermine the truism we teach our sophomores: that style and content are one. Both the name and the origin of the movement seem to imply that style is a separable entity, and the artists who participated in it display not only a new self-consciousness with style and a new mastery of it, but more—the seeds of self-parody. Friedlaender connects the sixteenth-century meaning of *maniera* with the sense of the cliché;[9] one might add the sense of satiety. Mannerism contains incipiently the materials for a critique of itself; it plays with the limits of stylistic flamboyance and sometimes deliberately transgresses them. At its most exuberant, it risks turning style into a scandal. Yet in the last analysis, it does not really refute the truism that style and content are inseparable. The weaker mannerist artists prove that truism by their very failure. The superior artists like Scève, and those greater than Scève, harness their stylistic liberties to the demands of their subject, demands that they intuit and satisfy at the sublest possible level. Even the most insistent style is docile enough in the hands of a master to support the burden of expression.

NOTES

Thomas M. Greene is Professor of Comparative Literature, Yale University. A somewhat altered version of this essay appears under the title "Styles of Experience in Scève's *Délie*," in *Image and Symbol in the Renaissance*, Yale French Studies, no. 47.

1. Sypher, *Four Stages of Renaissance Style* (Garden City, N.Y., 1955); Daniells, *Milton, Mannerism and Baroque* (Toronto, 1963).

2. Curtius, *European Literature and the Latin Middle Ages*, trans. Willard R. Trask (New York, 1953), pp. 273–301; Riccardo Scrivano, *Il manierismo nella letteratura del Cinquecento* (Padua, 1959); Georg Weise, "Manierismo e letteratura," *Rivista di letteratura moderne e comparate*, XIII (1960), 5–52; XIX (1966), 253–78; XXI (1968), 85–127; XXII (1969), 85–112; Marcel Raymond, "La Pléiade et le manièrisme," in *Lumières de la Pléiade*, ed. P. Mesnard (Paris, 1966).

3. "Laokoön: An Oracle Reconsulted," in *Eighteenth-Century Studies in Honor of Donald F. Hyde*, ed. William Bond (New York, 1970), p. 362.

4. "Second Thoughts on Currents and Periods," in *The Disciplines of Criticism*, ed. Peter Demetz, Thomas M. Greene, and Lowry Nelson, Jr. (New Haven, 1968), pp. 477–509.

5. *La magnificence de la superbe et triumphante entrée de la noble et antique Cité de Lyon faicte au Treschrestien Roy de France, Henri deuxième de ce nom. . .* (Lyon, 1549).

6. Curtius, pp. 275–78; Hatzfeld, "Mannerism Is not Baroque," *L'Esprit créateur*, VI (1966), 225–33.

7. All French quotations are from *The "Délie" of Maurice Scève*, ed. I. D. McFarlane (Cambridge, 1966). To facilitate reading, I have modernized the usage of *i*'s, *j*'s, *u*'s, and *v*'s. The number of the dizain from which a quotation is drawn follows in parentheses.

8. *Paradoxia epidemica* (Princeton, 1966), pp. 517–18.

9. Walter Friedlaender, *Mannerism and Anti-Mannerism in Italian Painting* (New York, 1957), page 48.

3

UT ORATORIA MUSICA:
THE RHETORICAL BASIS OF
MUSICAL MANNERISM

Claude V. Palisca

MANNERISM as a term denoting a stage in late Renaissance musical style or a transition to the baroque is enjoying a certain vogue in scholarly writings.[1] It is not being embraced, however, with the enthusiasm that the term *baroque* was forty years ago. Part of the reason is that we have become skeptical of all period divisions and blanket descriptions of them.

While in fields other than music enthusiasm for the term is also tempered with skepticism, music critics have a special reason to be hesitant in accepting new terms and concepts for musical phenomena. Every new critical insight or interpretation affects not only how music is heard but also how it is performed.

A new interpretation of early music thus transcends description to become potentially prescription. If a particular piece of music needs to be heard or understood a certain way, the performannce ought to facilitate that way of hearing and understanding it. Only the art of the theater shares this feature with music, but stage directors feel less compulsion to restore early theater to its original mode of performance and are therefore less affected by changes in critical understanding. Performing an early work of music with the media and practices of more recent music is judged rightly as a violation of its very nature and is consequently avoided. An analyst who introduces modern concepts into the interpretation of Renaissance music may be turning performers away from a faithful rendering of a piece as surely as if he counseled vibratos or animated crescendos where none were contemplated by the composer.

With this wide responsibility, the music critic enjoys the opportunity, not shared by art and literary critics, to hear his interpretations tested in performance. An anachronism will often be more glaringly exposed in the hearing of it than through intellectual reflection.

For these reasons it is perhaps more important to the music historian than to the art or literary historian whether mannerism is a concept imposed on the creative products of the late sixteenth century retrospectively or a quality consciously put there by their creators. The music critic, having experienced in falsified performances of early music the pitfalls of interpreting it by a methodology and esthetic standards of more recent times, will feel more comfortable with the term *mannerism* if it can be shown that mannerism was for a composer of the sixteenth century a conscious approach to his art. It is particularly apropos that this be shown in the case of mannerism, because if it is not conscious or even self-conscious, is it truly mannerism? To choose a manner or imitate one is a style-conscious act, whereas a personal musical style is the result of a multitude of decisions made quite independently of any concern for style.

If it could be shown that composers, musicians, and observers of the musical scene in the second half of the sixteenth century recognized the phenomenon that has come to be called mannerism, we would accept with greater confidence than we do now the existence of a mannerist period or style in the late Renaissance or early baroque. It would also add to our understanding of the relation of music to the other arts and to culture in general, because it would permit us to draw parallels, not by analogy, but through organic connections. The uncanny coincidence of mannerism in several arts at approximately the same time could be accounted for, not through evoking some illusory *Zeitgeist,* but by observing the transmission of ideas and techniques.

Neither the word *manierismo* nor its equivalent occurred in mid-sixteenth-century writings about music. But critics were conscious of a new departure, which they called *musica nuova, nuova maniera,* or *musica reservata.* As is often the case, we learn more about a new trend from its detractors than from its advocates.

Here is what one critic says about the new manners of composition in 1559 in a short section on music in a book on judiciary astrology. The author is Jean Taisnier, mathematician, doctor of laws, and choirmaster. In a digression from astrology, he announces that he is writing a book on the four mathematical disciplines in which he will treat music, both old and new. Of the new music, which he says some call *musica reservata,* he gives this opinion:

> And whenever they endeavor to contrive something new, disregarding in their compositions the modes that rest on the principles of music, they commit a great mistake; neglecting the ligatures of notes, their values in mode, tempus and prolation; [modulating], as they would have it (the expression is colloquial, for music, properly speaking, is not modulated), harmonious, flowing, running counterpoints in minims and semiminims, ad fugam, with repetitions, in perfect and imperfect modus, through major and minor hemiola, by sesquialtera, sesquitertia, sesquiquarta, etc.[2]

Here Taisnier recites a virtual catalogue of new manners: he notes the disregard for the limits of the modes of plainchant through chromatic intervals and alterations; he deplores the neglect of the proper proportions between shorter and longer notes, as through the sudden introduction of many notes of small value, such as semiminims in running passages of embellishment or counterpoint, and the changes from triple to duple meter and back; he complains of the abuse of fugue and its mixture with chordal declamatory passages and of repetitions, which were frowned upon in the idealized style of the textbooks.

Perceptive as Taisnier is about the properties of the new style, he shows no understanding of the motivation for the devices he enumerates, many being intended to imitate the meanings, feelings, and conceits of the texts set by the composers using them. To Taisnier the devices are distortions of the accepted and beautiful manner of writing (*bella maniera di scrivere*) such as taught by Gioseffo Zarlino.[3]

Taisnier became acquainted with the new style in two of the several breeding grounds of musical innovation—Rome and Naples—in the 1550s. In Rome a controversy flared up between the innovators and the defenders of the reigning practice. It is reflected in Nicola Vicentino's book, *The Ancient Music Reduced to the Modern Practice* of 1555.[4] Vicentino, who probably provoked Taisnier's tirade, gives us a key to what impelled composers to adopt certain of the devices: he counsels the composer to change the rate of movement of notes as a good orator would do:

> The movement of the measure should be changed to slower or faster according to the words. . . . The experience of the orator teaches us to do this, for in his oration he speaks now loudly, now softly, now slowly, now quickly, and thus greatly moves the listeners; and this manner of changing measure has great effect on the soul.[5]

Ut oratoria musica would have been a fitting motto of musical mannerism. There is hardly an author on music in the last half of the sixteenth century who does not dip into Quintilian's *Institutio oratoria*. It was one of the first printed books containing a discussion of music (Rome, 1470). It spread the idea that music is closely allied to oratory and that, like oratory, it has the function of moving listeners to various passions. In the section *De musica* (i.11) Quintilian pleads for music that excites generous feelings and calms disordered passions. In the section *De divisione affectuum et quomodo movendi sint* (vi.2) he classifies the affections and shows how the modulation of the voice differs according to the emotional circumstances of the speaker or character represented in a comedy or tragedy.

Despite the obvious links between music and oratory, no elaborate application of rhetorical theory to music appeared until 1599, and then not in Italy but in Germany. This was *Hypomnematum musicae poeticae . . . synopsis* [Notes for a synopsis of musical poetics] of Joachim Burmeister (ca. 1564–1629).[6] An elementary manual in musical composition written from a rhetorical slant, its approach was natural to an author brought up in the Latin school of the Lüneburg Johanneum, which had as the core of its curriculum the study of the Latin language, syntax, and rhetoric. After receiving the degree of *Magister* at the University of Rostock, Burmeister became cantor of St. Mary's, the university church, and teacher of Latin in the city's Collegium.

In the second (1601) edition of the book, under the title *Musica autoschediastike*, Burmeister eulogizes music as a higher form of oratory.

> In the art of oratory, insofar as it has power, that power resides not in the simple collection of simple words, in the proper measuring out of periods, and although they be plain, in their exquisite combination, which remains naked and always even and equal. Rather it resides in those things in which charm and elegance lie concealed in ornament and through words charged with wit, in periods enclosing a range of emphatic words. Thus also this art [music], beyond the naked mixture of perfect and imperfect consonances, offers to the sense through the intermingling of dissonances a combination that similarly cannot fail to touch the heart. . . . So that these things may deserve greater confidence, a single example may be selected from among many in the works of Orlandus [i.e., Lassus] in the song *Deus qui sedes* [*super thronum*] for five voices.[7] He interpreted the text "Laborem et dolorem, etc." so artfully; indeed he so portrayed it that through these very contorted inflections of intervals he put before the eyes the meaning of the thing [itself]. Certainly the mere regular interweaving of consonances does not accomplish this feat (*artificium*); rather the labor of craft and the learned syntax are swept away by the majesty of gesture and ornament. By Hercules, not Apelles, with the most accurate skill of his art, not Demosthenes, not Cicero by the art of persuading, deflecting, moving and orating, would have better placed the burden of trouble and lamentation before the eyes, moved the ears, implanted these [feelings] in the heart than Orlandus did with this harmonic art.[8]

Some years earlier (ca. 1560), the humanist Samuel Quickelberg (1529–68) also praised the power of Orlandus Lassus (1532–94) "to place the object almost alive before the eyes" ("rem quasi actam ante oculos ponendo"),[9] echoing the phrase "sub oculos subiiciendis" with which Quintilian describes the aim of the metaphor.[10] Another contemporary, the musician Gallus Dressler cited Lassus's "suavity and his skill in applying harmony to the words aptly and appropriately through ornament." [11]

Lassus was for Quickelberg a master of the music called *musica reservata* and for Burmeister the model of musical composition generally, just as Adrian Willaert had been the model of perfect counterpoint for Gioseffo Zarlino a generation earlier and Josquin des Prez for Heinrich Glarean some years before that. If Josquin represents a classical moment in the music of the sixteenth century, Lassus is the epitome of mannerism. Few composers were such masters as Lassus of the artifices of the composer-orator, and it is to Burmeister's credit that he identifies many of them, though we owe him little thanks, perhaps, for baptizing them with such names as *parrhesia* and *pleonasmus,* which to the non-rhetorician are more suggestive of fearful contagions than means of harmonic persuasion. Yet, insofar as a thing does not fully exist as a concept until it has been given a name, even Burmeister's pseudorhetorical terminology is better than none, and it has the advantage of descending from a venerable tradition.[12]

In a remarkable section of his *Musica autoschediastike* of 1601, expanded in his *Musica poetica* (1606),[13] Burmeister shows how one may construct with oratorical effect a sacred vocal composition by taking as a model the motet of Lassus, *In me transierunt.*[14] I know of no other place where an author of the sixteenth century takes us step by step through a work as Burmeister does here, and that within only a few years of the composer's death. In his analysis Burmeister shows that this motet is a quilt of rhetorical devices, and he identifies ten of them. Even so, he fails to note other devices that he names elsewhere in the treatises and overlooks some figures recognized by other authors.

The first step in the analysis of a composition, Burmeister instructs, is its division into periods, or "affections." He uses the terms *period* and *affection* interchangeably, for he defines musical affection (*affectio musica*) as "a period in melody or harmony terminated by a cadence that moves and affects the souls and hearts of men." [15] According to Burmeister's system, the periods of a composition, like those of an oration, fall into three main sections: the *exordium,* or introduction; the *corpus carminis,* the body of the song; and the *finis,* or conclusion.

In me transierunt of Lassus falls into nine periods, according to Burmeister.[16] They cover the following phrases of the text:

Exordium   1. In me transierunt irae tuae,
Confirmatio 2. et terrores tui
            3. conturbaverunt me:
            4. cor meum conturbatum est.
            5. Dereliquit me virtus mea.
            6. Dolor meus in conspectu meo semper.
            7. Ne derelinquas me
            8. Domine Deus meus;
Epilogue   9. ne discesseris a me.

Burmeister now analyzes each of the segments in terms of the rhetoricomusical figures it contains. In the examples that follow, figures pointed out in Burmeister's analysis or elsewhere in his treatises are given in boxes ☐, figures

named by Burmeister in his treatises but not specifically related to this example
are given in square brackets [ ], and figures not recognized by Burmeister are
given in curved braces ⌣⌣.

Exordium, Period 1. Measures 1 to 20. (Ex. 1)

Burmeister identifies this passage as an *exordium* with double ornament,
meaning that there are two figures present: *fuga realis* and *hypallage*. By *fuga
realis* is meant the texture in which every voice of a harmony after the first
imitates the melody stated in the first voice through the same or similar intervals.
Here the Altus imitates the Cantus by contrary motion (*hypallage*), except that
the first note is transposed an octave down. This alteration of the subject gives
this opening something of the character of a double fugue (*metalepsis*), particularly
since the Bass in measure 4 imitates the Altus exactly. The other voices have the
subject in direct motion.

The *exordium* includes several figures that Burmeister points out as occurring
in this motet, not in the analysis itself, but in other places in the treatise or in
previous versions of the treatise. On the word "irae" ("wrath") in the Cantus
(mm. 4–5) Lassus employs a *hypobole,* which Burmeister defines as a trans-
gression of the lower limit of the ambitus of a mode, the mode in this case
being Phrygian E to E.[17] Measures 4 to 7 of the Tenor 1 and Bass are used to
illustrate the *parrhesia* in *Musica autoschediastike.*[18] A *parrhesia* is defined as "a
mixture among other consonances of a single dissonance of the value of half of a
tactus [*tactus* = semibreve or a half measure in the transcription]." [19] The
parrhesia is a special case of the *maius symblema,* a dissonance on the second part
of a half measure worth a minim, or half note, of which there are numerous
examples in this motet.[20]

Burmeister does not bother to point out the *syncopa,* or *syneresis,* a figure he
describes as a dissonance in the beginning of a *tactus* that is bound to a sound that
enters by syncopation in the preceding *tactus* and must be resolved (*dissoluta esse
deberent*) in a consonance—the suspension of modern theory.[21] A more significant omission is the unorthodox leap of a minor sixth, frowned upon by the
counterpoint rule books, with which the subject begins.

Oddly, Burmeister also says nothing about an important ornament occurring
in measures 6 to 7, the evaded cadence. On the other hand, this device was
recognized as a figure by Francis Bacon in 1605 in a passage apparently overlooked by musical scholars in the *Advancement of Learning.* Bacon's discussion
of musical figures is worth quoting in full, as it seems quite independent of
known Continental sources.

> Is not the precept of a Musitian, to fall from a discord or harsh accord, vpon
> a concord, or sweete accord, alike true affection? Is not the Trope of
> Musicke, to auoyde or slyde from the close or Cadence, common with the

Example 1: Orlandus Lassus, In me transierunt, *mm. 1–20*

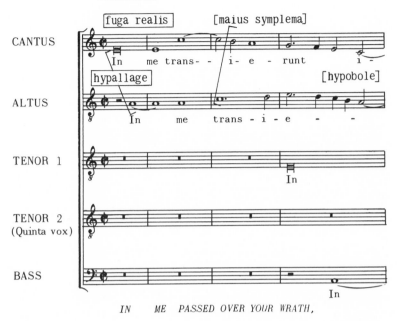

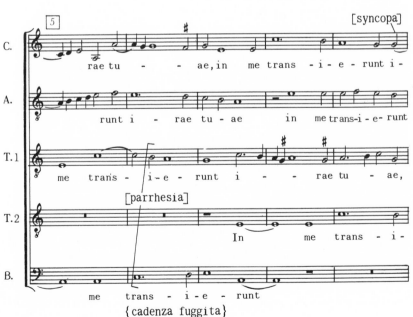

Trope of Rhetoricke of deceyuing expectation? Is not the delight of the Quavering vppon a stoppe in Musique, the same with the playing of Light vppon the water?

Splendet tremulo sub Lumine Pontus

Are not the Organs of the senses of one kinde with the Organs of Reflexion, the Eye with a glasse, the Eare with a Caue or Straight determined and bounded? Neither are these onely similitudes, as men of narrowe observation may conceyue them to bee, but the same footsteppes of Nature, treading or printing vppon seuerall subiects or Matters.[22]

This plea for a comprehensive examination of the uniformity of nature is expanded in the *De dignitate et augmentis scientiarum libros IX* of 1623, and at the same time its language is clarified:

Tropus ille Musicus, *à clausulâ* aut *Cadentiâ* (quam vocant) cùm iam-iam *adesse videatur, placidè elabendi;* conuenit cum Tropo Rhetorico *Expectationem eludendi. Fidium sonus tremulus,* eandem affert auribus voluptatem, quam Lumen, Aquae aut Gemmae insiliens, Oculis . . .[23]

"To auoyde or slyde from the close or Cadence" and "Cadentiâ . . . placidè elabendi" obviously refer to the deceptive or evaded cadence that Zarlino describes as "fuggire la cadenza," and Thomas Morley, as "false closes." [24] It is significant that an anonymous author in France, writing of musical figures somewhere between 1559 and 1571, singles out the evaded cadence as a favorite device of *musica reservata*.[25] Lassus and other masters of the new music depended greatly on the evaded cadence, which permitted them to break up their texts into short phrases for descriptive and affective emphasis, while maintaining harmonic continuity.

Bacon's expression "Fidium sonus tremulus" of the Latin version helps us identify the "Quavering vppon a stoppe in Musique" of the 1605 text as the vibrato, used at this time as an ornament in the playing of string instruments.

Bacon's first device, "to fall from a discord or harsh accord, vpon a concord," is Burmeister's *syneresis,* the suspension.

In *Sylva sylvarum,* published in 1627 after Bacon's death, the discussion of musical devices is integrated into section 113 of Century Two and is expanded at the end to include several more devices used by Lassus and his contemporaries. Now all of the devices he mentioned earlier are included among the figures, or tropes, of musical rhetoric: vibrato, division (perhaps meaning diminutions of longer notes through trills and other ornaments), suspension, evaded cadence, fugue, and change from duple to triple and back.

There be in *Musick* certaine *Figures,* or *Tropes;* almost agreeing with the *Figures* of *Rhetoricke;* And with the *Affections* of the *Minde,* and other

Senses: First, the *Diuision* and *Quauering* . . . [The passage omitted here is very close to the version of 1605.] The *Reports,* and *Fuges,* have an Agreement with the *Figures* in *Rhetorik* [*sic*], of *Repetition,* and *Traduction.* The *Tripla's,* and *Changing of Times,* haue an Agreement with the *Changes of Motions;* As when *Galliard Time,* and *Measure Time,* are in the *Medley* of one Dance.[26]

The progression of Bacon's thought from a recognition of the analogy between musical effects and the movements of the affections toward the identification of musical devices with the tropes, or figures, of rhetoric shows a growing awareness of the part musical artifices play in musical expression. Bacon's struggle for appropriate terms leads us to the conclusion that he arrived at this parallel of music and rhetoric through an independent observation of the ways of musical mannerism, which abounds in the Elizabethan and Jacobean madrigals, motets, and anthems.

Confirmatio. Period 2. Measures 20–26. (Ex. 2)

Burmeister likens the main body of the composition to the confirmation of an

Example 2: Lassus, In me transierunt, *mm. 20–26*

oration. The text of this central part of the work, he says, is impressed on the minds of the listeners in a manner similar to that of the confirming arguments of oratory.

The second period is adorned, Burmeister writes, with *hypotyposis, climax,* and *anadiplosis. Hypotyposis* "is that ornament by which the significance of a text is so delineated that the music near the text is seen to acquire life." Here is Quintilian's *sub oculis subiicere.* The syncopated repeated notes of "et terrores tui" send a shiver through the voice parts like a spreading panic. At the same time the *climax,* a repetition of the same motive in stepwise progression in the Bass, gives a sinking feeling. The texture of the four upper parts is subtly interwoven out of interlocking voice pairs, each pair being immediately imitated by another, the technique called *anadiplosis,* which will be more clearly illustrated in the third period.

Period 3. Measures 26–32. (Ex. 3)

The parallel motion of measure 27 was considered out of style and cautioned against by Zarlino in 1558.[27] It was probably considered undesirable for the very

Example 3: Lassus, In me transierunt, *mm. 26–32*

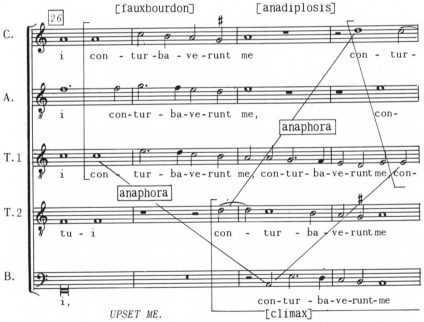

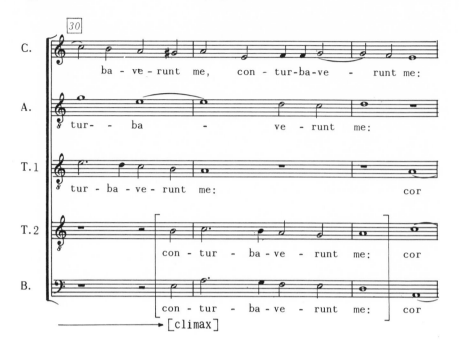

reason it is effective here: it gives one the disconcerting feeling that the bottom has dropped out. Thus it illustrates perfectly the words "conturbaverunt me" ("they upset me"). Burmeister elsewhere calls this figure *fauxbourdon,* the traditional name for the harmony of parallel sixths and thirds frequently improvised in the fifteenth century. As in period 2, the texture may be analyzed as a set of interlocking imitations among several voice groups (*anadiplosis*) in the succession Cantus–Altus–Tenor 1, Tenor 2–Bass, Cantus–Tenor 1, Tenor 2–Bass. Burmeister notes the presence of *anaphora,* or partial fugue, involving, that is, fewer than the full number of parts, in this case only two voice pairs: Tenor 1–Bass, measures 26–29; and Tenor 2–Cantus, measures 27–31.

Period 4. Measures 32–45. (Ex. 4)

Measure 33 introduces the most dramatic change in the piece. The movement slows down from a predominance of half notes to the rhythm of the whole note (the semibreve, or unit of *tactus*).[28] The voices, alternating ties and attacks, produce a throbbing effect to represent the beating of the heart, a vivid *hypotyposis.* It is probably not incidental here that the rate of time beating around 1560, when the semibreve was the unit of beat in ¢, was defined as the pulse of a man at rest. Thus the alternating voices are like the systole and diastole of the

Example 4: Lassus, In me transierunt, *mm. 32–41*

Example 5: Lassus, In me transierunt, mm. 41–46

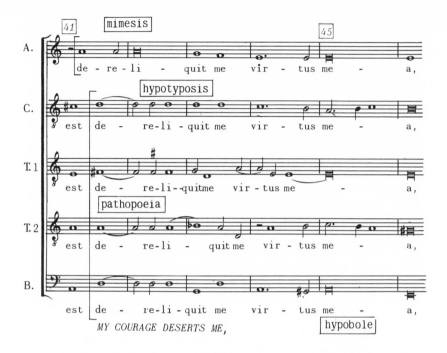

heart, to which Zarlino likened the down-beat and up-beat of the measure.[29] The "cor meum" section also illustrates the device of *auxesis*, which Burmeister defines as occurring "when a harmony made up only of consonances under one and the same text while being repeated once, twice, or three times or more, grows and rises." [30] The "cor meum" harmony rises an octave under the same text.

The phrase "conturbatum est" ("is troubled"), which Burmeister seems to consider as part of the same period, literally disrupts the restful beating of the heart with its syncopations and contorted bass melody, descending by way of a *climax*, while the homophonic group of measures 36–38, Altus, Tenor 1 and 2, and Bass, is answered through the device of *mimesis* by the highest four voices, then again by the lowest four.

Period 5. Measures 41–46. (Ex. 5)

The phrase "dereliquit me virtus mea" ("my courage deserts me") introduces a new figure, *pathopoeia*, "apt for arousing an affection, which is accomplished by introducing into the song semitones that do not belong to the mode or genus of the song." [31] The F-sharp in the Tenor 1 of measure 41 is external to the Phrygian mode, as is the B-flat in Tenor 2 in measure 43, the two producing a false-relation, a device that somehow escaped Burmeister's roster. *Hypotyposis* is again present, as Burmeister notes, in the descending line of the Cantus and in the *hypobole* of the Bass, which reaches below the modal ambitus in an image of despair.[32]

Period 6. Measures 46–67. (Ex. 6)

The only figure Burmeister identifies in this segment is the *fuga realis*, which begins at measure 52 in Tenor 2 at the words "in conspectu meo semper" ("is continually before me"). The fugue subject is, indeed, ever before us, being repeated nine times in fifteen measures. But there are several other notable usages: half-step motion in the Cantus, inverted in the Tenor 2, expresses the feeling of "dolor meus," as does the *pathopoeia* through the added B-flat in Tenor 1 and Bass. *Congeries,* "an accumulation of perfect and imperfect consonant intervals, the movement of which is permitted [by the rules of counterpoint]," lends a harmonic fullness and sweetness to measures 46–49 and 52–53.[33] At the end of the fugue, at measures 66–67, a figure that is the antithesis of *congeries,* an accumulation of dissonances over three beats (triple *pleonasmus*), brings the fugue to a close.[34]

Example 6: Lassus, In me transierunt, *mm. 46–67*

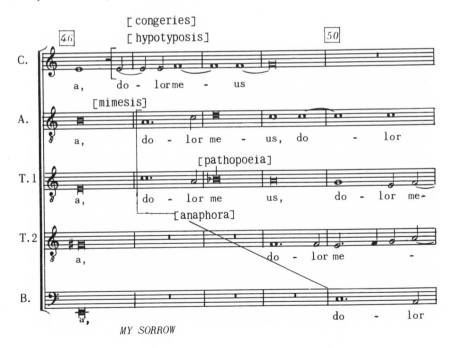

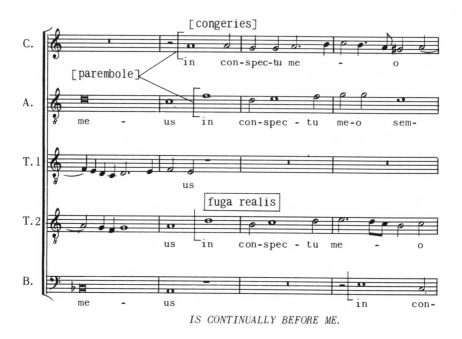

IS CONTINUALLY BEFORE ME.

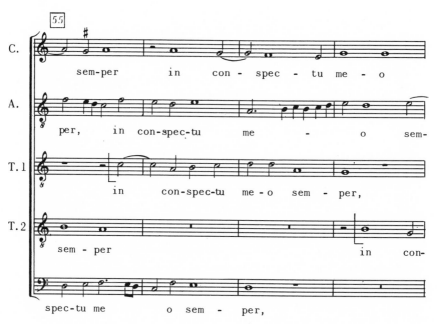

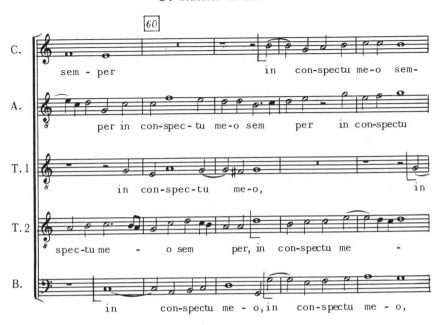

sem - per ... in con-spectu me-o sem-
per in con-spec-tu me-o sem per in con-spectu
in con-spec-tu me-o, in
spec-tu me - o sem per, in con-spectu me -
in con-spectu me - o, in con-spectu me - o,

[pleonasmus sub triplici tactu]

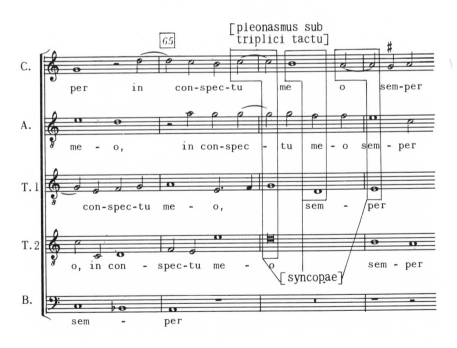

per in con-spec-tu me o sem-per
me - o, in con-spec - tu me - o sem - per
con-spec-tu me - o, sem - per
o, in con - spec-tu me - o sem - per
[syncopae]
sem - per

Example 7: Lassus, In me transierunt, *mm. 67–73*

Period 7. Measures 67–73. (Ex. 7)

After the *fuga realis* the sudden change to homophonic declamatory style (*noema*) is meant to attract the listener's attention to the plea "ne derelinquas me" ("forsake me not"). The insecurity of the psalmist is characterized by the displacement of normal accents: the accented syllable *lin* of *derelinquas* falls almost each time on the second half of the beat. The pleading is made insistent with the use of *pallilogia,* repetition of a melodic phrase at the original tonal level (mm. 67–68 and 71–73 in the Bass).

Period 8. Measures 73–77. (Ex. 8)

The displacement of the accented syllables persists in the *noema* on the words "Domine Deus meus." Only the Tenor 2 hits *Do* of *Domine* on the beat. This distortion of the normal meter insinuates in the listener again the uneasiness of the psalmist.

Example 8: Lassus, In me transierunt, *mm. 73–77*

Epilogue. Period 9. Measures 78–87. (Ex. 9)

The close employs several rhetorical devices of repetition: the repetition of a motive in the Bass a tone higher (*climax,* mm. 78–80, 84–86); the corresponding repetition in the same place of a chordal section on the same text at a new level (*auxesis*); and the thrice-repeated sequence of notes in the Cantus, C–B–A–G-sharp–A, in measures 81–82, 82–83, 86–87, the last time varied, which constitutes a *pallilogia.* The composition seems to come to a close on measure 84 but is extended for a fuller close through four measures of *supplementum.* This Burmeister describes as "the principal close, in which either the entire part-movement (*modulatio*) comes to a standstill or two voices or one holds fast while others scatter yet a small amount of melody. . . . It is placed there so that it might penetrate the mind of the hearers more clearly by moving as the end approaches." [35]

This brings us to the end of Burmeister's analysis, which is given verbatim in translation in the appendix at the end of this article. What is the significance of this analysis from the standpoint of mannerism?

Burmeister's purpose was to call attention to certain manners of composition so that young composers might imitate them. "The separation of a song into affections is the division of the song into periods or affections for the sake of inquiring into the device (*artificium*) and for the sake of transforming it by imitation." [36] A vocal composition is conceived as a collection of periods, each contrived by means of some artifice or more than one. Each period represents a distinct affection through some manner inspired by the text.

However, not every device considered by Burmeister is expressive or has an expressive purpose. Many of them are simply constructive devices, artifices that grew out of a need to knit together the voices of a composition once the *cantus firmus* was abandoned as the main thread earlier in the century. The words *musica poetica* in Burmeister's title do not signify the art of poetic music or musical poetry, as some have inferred, but the art of making (from the Greek *poiein*) musical compositions: "Musica poetica est ars quae *Melodias et Harmonias* docet effingere et componere." [37] *Fuga, mimesis, anadiplosis, hypallage,* and *anaphora* are various ways of interrelating the parts of a polyphonic composition. *Climax* and *auxesis* are means of achieving continuity. They are artfully disguised repetitions that permit the total sound to be renewed while details are being reused. The level of redundancy essential to musical coherence would be intolerable in prose, even in oratory. Consequently, music is a natural sanctuary for the rhetorical figures that involve repetition.[38]

Whether for reasons of artful construction or expression, a composition is strung out of devices or disparate manners of artful writing. The listener's attention at any moment is drawn to details, clever conceits that are integrated into the whole intellectually, not aurally as a flow of sound. There is less danger

Example 9: Lassus, In me transierunt, *mm. 78–87*

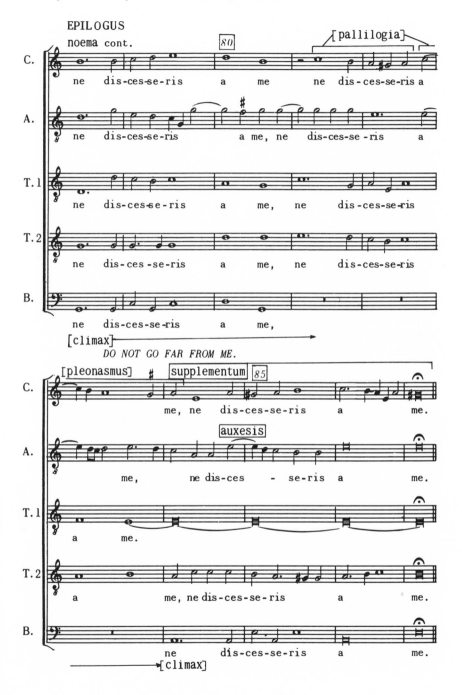

in music than in prose or poetry of losing continuity, because by its nature music
moves on, impelled forward by the momentum of rhythm, the expectation of
consonance after dissonance, the curve of the melodic line, and the march to the
cadence. Laymen listening to *In me transierunt* may even be oblivious to the
scattering effect of the succession of manners—particularly modern listeners,
conditioned as they are by the variety of colors of instrumental music and accompanied vocal music. Many of the details must have escaped the notice of
Lassus's contemporaries, too; this artful music was addressed more to singers,
amateurs, and patrons than to church-going worshippers.

This music is for an in-group, one that understands Latin, is sensitive to
the constructivist devices, recognizes the allusions, and enjoys mixed-media puns
with words, sounds, and musical notation—it is, in a word, a *musica reservata*. It
is not plain, transparent music, as Burmeister states in his preface to *Musica
autoschediastike*, but elegant and artful. What Lorenzo Giacomini, a lover of
music as well as a literary critic, says of Tasso applies as well to Lassus:

> To consider first the beauty of style, he is not surpassed by any of the ancients
> or moderns in the choice of words—grave, sweet, harsh, sonorous, splendid,
> imperious—and in the loftiness and abundance of ornaments. And in those
> three [ornaments] to which the orator must particularly aim was he taught
> by the Master of all knowledge? Realizing that the Tuscan language, be-
> cause it is sweeter than the Latin and less sonorous, needs a great boost of
> magnificence; recognizing that extreme clarity is but excessive ease of being
> immediately understood without giving the listener a chance to learn any-
> thing by himself, which, when joined by vulgarity and baseness, produces
> contempt and not pleasure in the alert listener, who disdains being treated as
> a child; with assiduous attention he banished from his poems loftiness, ef-
> ficiency, and excellent grace, but not supreme clarity—not the clarity ap-
> propriate to that genre of speech, which, provided it reaches well the intellect,
> the end of all speech, avoids that excessive ease of being too quickly understood,
> and, departing from the customary, the humble and lowly, loves the new, the
> unused, the unexpected, the admirable, both in conceits and words. His words,
> interwoven with more artifice than in common speech, are adorned with
> a variety of figures apt for tempering that excessive clarity, such as interrup-
> tions, inversions, circumlocutions, hyperbole, irony, transpositions, and those
> that derive from the whole and the part, and the cause and effect. [His
> diction] thus is made to resemble not the winding, level, and muddy public
> alleys but the steep and rocky paths where the weak are exhausted and the
> unwary stumble. This manner of speaking—noble, rare, and remote from
> that understood by commoners—was assumed and followed by those famous
> sagas, which hence were told in a language other than that of usual speech.
> . . . . If we examine the conceits, we shall find them noble, vivid, apt for
> exciting the affections where and to the degree required, gracious, sharp, so

that they have the power to keep the intellect of the listener alert and to stimulate him to press on.[39]

Like Tasso, Lassus avoids the transparent, plain, and uniform style of his predecessors and seeks constantly the unexpected, clever turns that inspire wonder and test the ingenuity of the listener to penetrate the thought and follow the thread of the music. In the lofty style of the late sixteenth-century motet and madrigal, as with the poetry of Tasso, the musician dons the toga of the orator and equips himself from the armory of devices catalogued by Burmeister.

If musical mannerism was the product of the oratorical impulse of the mid-sixteenth century, it was also a cul de sac, because the means were not equal to the end, which was to move listeners the way an orator or preacher moves his audience. Mannerism was a stage on the way to fulfilling this aspiration. The true *stilus oratoricus* was the recitative style, which rewarded a renewed search for an adequate manner toward the end of the sixteenth century. In this mannerism was a search, the baroque a fulfillment.

APPENDIX

Here follows the entire analysis of *In me transierunt* of Lassus by Joachim Burmeister, as translated from *Musica poetica* (Rostock, 1606), cap. 15, pp. 73–74.[1]

This elegant and splendid composition, *In me transierunt*, by Orlandus Lassus is bounded by the Phrygian authentic mode.[2] The ambitus covers the entire system of steps, from [low] B-natural to e.[3] The ambitus of the single voices is as follows: the Discantus, from e to e; the Tenor, from E to e; the Bass from B-natural to b-natural; the Altus from b-natural to b-natural.[4] The basic temperament is Orthian or authentic. The interval of the fifth from E to ♮ [b] is manifested. Later there is introduced a *clausula affinalis* where this fifth is divided into two equal parts, in place of the full or *echaphone* (ἐχάφῶνε) close, which is usually formed there. The ambitus of the Altus and Bass voices is plagal. Where cadences lead to a full close, that is *trepsonor* (τρεψωνῶρ), they are formed in a manner accepted through long use, with the ambitus of the lower voice mediated by a fourth, that of the higher voice by a fifth. Semitones appear in both their locations. The lower place of the semitone is the first interval of the authentic ambitus. The higher place is plainly the same as the lower place, etc. The composition ends in E authentic, which is the customary lowest sound of the ambitus of the tenor.[5] Secondly, it belongs to the diatonic genus of melody, the intervals of which are formed mainly by tone, tone, and semitone. Thirdly, it belongs to the genus of broken [mensural] antiphons (*antiphonarum fractum*) [i.e., diminished or florid counterpoint]. The notes are mixed with each other in unequal values. Fourthly, it has the quality of the Diezeugmenon. In the whole chant the disjunction of the tetrachords occurs between a and b.

Moreover this composition may be divided conveniently into nine periods. The first contains the *exordium*, which is an *exordium* with double ornament, one of which is a *fuga realis*, the other a *hypallage*. The seven internal [periods] are the body of the composition and are equivalent to the *confirmatio* in an oration (if one may be permitted to compare thus one art to a cognate art). Of these [seven periods] the first is adorned with a *hypotyposis*, a *climax*, and an *anadiplosis*. The second similarly, and in addition an *anaphora* may be added. The third: *hypotyposis* and *mimesis*; the fourth in a similar way, and besides a *pathopoeia*; the fifth a *fuga realis*; the sixth an *anadiplosis* and *noema*; the seventh *noema* and *mimesis*. The last, that is the ninth period, is like the *epilogue* in an oration. The composition has a principal close, arrived at through harmonies in keeping with the nature of the mode, to which the composition returns and is accustomed to touch again and again along with foreign harmonies, sometimes called the supplement of the final cadence, which bears very frequently the ornament *auxesis*.

NOTES TO APPENDIX

1. The footnotes show essential variants in the *Musica autoschediastike*, 1601.

2. ". . . is in the diatonic genre, since the intervals employed proceed by tone and semitone. It is determined to be in the Phrygian authentic mode."

3. "The system goes from A to e."

4. "The Bass from A and a; the Altus from a to a. The mediation of the Discant and Tenor is authentic."

5. The passage from here to the end of the paragraph is missing.

NOTES

Claude V. Palisca is Professor of the History of Music, Yale University.

1. Robert E. Wolf, "The Aesthetic Problem of the Renaissance," *Revue belge de musicologie*, IX (1955), 83–102, and "Renaissance, Mannerism, Baroque," *Colloques de Wégimont*, IV (1957) (Paris, 1963), 35–80; Claude V. Palisca, "A Clarification of 'Musica Reservata' in Jean Taisnier's 'Astrologiae,' 1559," *Acta musicologica*, XXI (1959), 133–61; Beekman C. Cannon, Alvin Johnson, and William G. Waite, *The Art of Music* (New York, 1960); Henry W. Kaufmann, *The Life and Works of Nicola Vicentino* (Rome, 1960); James Haar, "Classicism and Mannerism in Sixteenth-Century Music," *The International Review of Music Aesthetics and Sociology*, I (Zagreb, 1970), 55–67; Don Harran, "'Mannerism' in the Cinquecento Madrigal?" *Musical Quarterly*, LV (1969), 521–44; Maria R. Maniates, "Musical Mannerism: Effeteness or Virility?" *Musical Quarterly*, LVII (1971), 270–93.

2. *Astrologiae ivdiciariae ysagogica* (Cologne, 1559), pp. 14–16; translated in Palisca, "A Clarification of 'Musica Reservata,' " p. 141.

3. *Le istitutioni harmoniche* (Venice, 1558).

4. *L'antica musica ridotta alla moderna prattica* (Rome, 1555).

5. *Ibid.*, IV, xxxxii, fol. 94v. Except where indicated otherwise, all translations are mine.

6. *Hypomnematum musicae poeticae, ex Isagoge cujus & idem ipse auctor est, ad chorum gubernandum, cantumque componendum conscriptam, synopsis* (Rostock, 1599). Burmeister published two considerably revised versions of this treatise: *Musica αὐτοσχεδιαστικὴ quae per aliquot accessiones in gratiam philomusorum quorundam ad Tractatum de Hypomnematibus Musicae Poëticae ejusdem auctoris σπωράδιω quondam exaratas, in unum corpusculum concrevit, in quâ redditur ratio I. Formandi & compoendi Harmonias; II. Administrandi & regendi Chorum; III. Canendi Melodias modo hactenùs non usitatô* (Rostock, 1601), and *Musica poetica: Definitionibus et divisionibus breviter delineata, quibus in singulis capitibus sunt hypomnemata praeceptionum instar συνοπτικῶσ addita, edita studiô & operâ M. Joachimi Burmeisteri, Lunaeburg. Scholae Rostoch. Collegae Classici* (Rostock, 1606; fac. ed. Kassel and Basel, 1955).

Other German authors had noted relationships between rhetorical principles and musical composition, but they had tended to be analogical, such as Georg Rhau's comparison between the eight parts of an oration and the eight modes of music (*Enchiridion utriusque Musicae Practicae* [Wittenberg, 1538], cap. 4) and Sebald Heyden's between grammatical signs and the various signs used in musical notation (*De arte canendi* [Nuremberg, 1540]). Of the early authors only Gallus Dressler describes the task of musical composition in rhetorical terms: cadences on various tones of the mode are like comma, accent, and period (*comma, virgula, periodus*); pauses are inserted in music for emphasis, as at the name Jesus Christ in a motet, but also for elegance and suavity (*Praecepta musicae poeticae* [Magdeburg, 1563]). Clemens non Papa excels in the use of three ornaments in particular—syncopation, *vicinae clausulae*, and fugues. Dressler speaks of the *exordium*, middle, and end of a composition. These and other examples of rhetorical terms and concepts applied to music are given in an anthology of quotations in Martin Ruhnke, *Joachim Burmeister: Ein Beitrag zur Musiklehre um 1600* (Kassel and Basel, 1955), pp. 135–38.

7. Orlandus Lassus, *Sacrae cantiones quinque vocum* (Nuremberg, 1562); modern edition in Orlando di Lasso, *Sämtliche Werke*, ed. Franz X. Haberl, XIX (Leipzig, 1908), 12–14.

8. Burmeister, *Musica autoschediastike*, fols. A2v–A3. For the Latin text, see Burmeister, *Musica poetica*, fac. ed., *Nachwort* by Martin Ruhnke.

9. Adolf Sandberger, *Beiträge zur Geschichte der bayerischen Hofkapelle unter Orlando di Lasso* (Leipzig, 1894–95), I, 56, n.2. My translation of the full passage is in "A Clarification of 'Musica Reservata,' " p. 154.

10. *Inst. orat.* viii. 6. 19.

11. *Praecepta musicae poeticae*, cap. 15, quoted in Ruhnke, *Joachim Burmeister*, p. 137.

12. The fullest and best illustrated discussions of the musical figures are in the first two versions of the treatise: *Hypomnematum musicae poeticae*, cap. 12, fols. G2–I1v, and *Musica autoschediastike*, cap. 12, fols. G1–L4. In the first of these the musical examples are in a special letter notation; in the second version, in mensural notation. *Musica poetica*, cap. 12, pp. 60–70, omits most of the examples, and the definitions of the terms are abridged. Burmeister names twenty-five figures altogether. Most of Burmeister's terms are borrowed directly from the rhetorical treatises, particularly from Lucas Lossius, *Erotemata dialecticae et rhetoricae Philippi Melanchtonis* (Leipzig, 1562). See Ruhnke, *Joachim Burmeister*, pp. 147–60. However, a number of the terms are of his own coinage, a process he defends by the authority of Quintilian (*Inst. Orat.* viii. 3), who cited the Greeks as not averse to forming new words rather than continuing to labor under the poverty of language (*Musica autoschediastike*, fol. A3v–4).

13. Burmeister, *Musica autoschediastike*, fols. L4–M1, end of cap. 12; *Musica poetica*, cap. 15, pp. 71–74, see translation of entire chapter in appendix to this essay.

14. *Sacrae cantiones quinque vocum*; (Nuremberg, 1562); *Sämtliche Werke*, IX, 49–52.

15. Burmeister, *Musica autoschediastike*, fol. O2v.

16. An analysis more attentive to the musical structure would produce eleven divisions:

		Psalms
Exordium	1. In me transierunt irae tuae,	87:17a
Confirmatio	2. et terrores tui ⎫	17b
	3. conturbaverunt me: ⎭	
	4. cor meum ⎫	37:11a
	5. conturbatum est. ⎭	
	6. Dereliquit me virtus mea.	11b
	7. Dolor meus ⎫	18b
	8. in conspectu meo semper. ⎭	
	9. Ne derelinquas me ⎫	22a
	10. Domine Deus meus; ⎭	
Epilogue	11. ne discesseris a me.	22b

The text is split into even smaller segments than Burmeister acknowledges, if the cadences in Lassus's motet are really taken as the criterion for defining preiods, as Burmeister instructs. (In *Musica poetica*, cap. 5, he implies that a period, or affection, is a section between two cadences.) Whereas a composer of the early sixteenth century would have observed the integrity of the half-verses, Lassus splits the verbal message of three and a half psalm verses into eleven segments, each of which carries its separate musical message and is composed in a different manner.

17. Burmeister, *Musica poetica*, p. 64.

18. Fol. L2v.

19. Burmeister, *Musica poetica*, p. 64.

20. The *minus symblema*, of the value of less than a half *tactus*, that is a quarter note or less, on the other hand, is not reputed to be an ornament or figure, Burmeister maintains, because it does not affect the hearing significantly (*Musica poetica*, p. 60).

21. *Ibid.*

22. *The Tvvoo Bookes Of the Proficiencie and Aduancement of Learning diuine and humane.* (London, 1605), fols. 21v–22r.

23. *Opera Franscisci baronis de Vervlamio, tomvs primvs* (London, 1624), III, cap. i, p. 139.

24. "Being devised to shun a final end and go on with some other purpose" (Thomas Morley, ed. R. Alec Harman, *A Plain and Easy Introduction to Practical Music* [1597] [London, 1952], III, 223).

25. Anonymous, *De musica*, in Johann F. Schannat and Joseph Hartzheim, eds., *Concilia Germaniae* (Cologne, 1759–75), VIII, 203–8. See Palisca, "A Clarification of 'Musica Reservata,'" p. 156.

26. *Sylva sylvarum: or A naturall historie. In ten centvries.* (London, 1627), p. 38.

27. *Istitutioni*, III, lxv, tr. by Guy A. Marco and Claude V. Palisca in Zarlino, *The Art of Counterpoint, Part III of 'Le Istitutioni harmoniche,' 1558* (New Haven, 1968), pp. 194–95.

28. Some modern authors use the term *tactus* to signify unit of measure, as in the German *Takt*. By *tactus* Burmeister means the beat, of which there are two to the meausre. In ¢ the beat is on the semibreve, and there are two semibreves to the measure, totaling a breve, hence *misura alla breve*.

29. *The Art of Counterpoint*, p. 117.

30. Burmeister, *Musica poetica*, p. 61.

31. *Ibid.*

32. Burmeister cites this passage as an example of the *hypobole* in his definition (*ibid.*, p. 64).

33. *Ibid.*, p. 65.

34. The *pleonasmus* is defined as "an abundance of harmony that in the formation of the cadence, particularly in its middle [i.e., between the preparation and the resolution], is made up of symblemas and syncopas, over two, three, or more half-measures" (*ibid.*, p. 61).

35. *Ibid.*, p. 73.

36. *Ibid.*, p. 71.

37. Burmeister, *Musica autoschediastike*, fol. N2.

38. Burmeister was able to borrow from rhetoric a number of the terms for figures of repetition: *anadiplosis*, in rhetoric the repetition of the last word of a period to initiate a new period, in music is the answering of one *mimesis* by another; *pallilogia*, in rhetoric the repetition of a word as opposed to a phrase, in music is a simple repetition of a series of pitches; *anaphora*, in rhetoric the repetition of the same word at the beginning of several periods, in music is the imitation of a musical subject in only some of the voice parts.

39. *Oratione in lode di Torquato Tasso* (Florence, 1596), pp. 14–17:

. . . (per considerare primieramente la bellezza de lo stile) da nessuno da gli antichi o de moderni riman vinto, ne la elezzione de le parole graui dolci aspre sonore splendide signoreggianti, e nel altezza e nel abondanza degli ornamenti, e in quei tre segnatamente, a quali douer sempre hauere la mira il dicitore, dal Maestro d'ogni dottrina fu insegnato? Egli considerando la Toscan fauella come de la Latina più dolce cosi meno sonora grandi aiuti per la magnificenza ricercare, e conoscendo la estrema chiarezza, la quale altro non è, che soprabondante ageuolezza di troppa subita intelligenza senza dare spazio al ascoltante d'imparare alcuna cosa da se medesimo, hauer congiunta seco viltà, e bassezza, e produrre dispregio e non aggradire al accorto vditore, ilquale si sdegna di esser fanciullescamente trattato, con sollecito studio procacciò a suoi poemi altezza efficacia e leggiadra eccellente, ma non somma chiarezza; tale nondimeno, quale conuiene a quella forma di parlare, che ben consegue la intelligenza fine d'ogni parlare, ma sfugge quella soverchia ageuolezza d'esser tosto inteso, & allontanandosi dal vsitato dal humile e dal abbietto, ama il nuouo il disusato l'inaspettato l'ammirabile, si ne concetti si ne le parole; Le quali mentre fuor del vulgare vso artifiziosamente intreccia, e mentre le adorna di varie figure atte a temperare quell'eccesso di chiarezza Troncamenti Strauolgimenti Circonscrizioni Hiperbole Ironie Translazioni, e quelle che da' luoghi del Tutto e de la Parte, de la Cagione e degli Effetti traggono origine, si rende simigliante non a le pubbliche stradechine e sdruccioleuoli o piane e fangose, ma a gli erti e sassosi sentieri, oue i piu debili sogliono stancarsi, & i men cauti talor inciampare. La quale maniera di dire nobile peregrina e rimota da la vulgare intelligenza, fu amata e seguita da que' famosi saggi, i quali perciò furono detti in altra lingua lor proprio hauer fauellato. . . . Ma se riguardiamo i Concetti, gli trouerremo nobili viui atti ad eccitare affetti doue e quanto bisogna, graziosi, acuti, si che hanno forza di tenere desto l'Intelletto del vditore, e di sospingerlo a considerare più auanti.

4

MANIERA AND THE MANNAIA: DECORUM AND DECAPITATION IN THE SIXTEENTH CENTURY

Samuel Y. Edgerton, Jr.

CONSIDER that the practice of public execution in the sixteenth century could be matter for mannerist esthetics.

Eschatology has always furnished poignant material to art and literature. People of all times and places, it seems, have been morbidly fascinated by the image of the condemned man taking his final journey to death. Public execution with its attendant dramatic intensity has in every age been turned into a styled occasion in order to impress upon the populace a didactic message concerning the wages of sin. So it has been true in almost every human culture since the beginning of man's presence on earth.

During the fourteenth and fifteenth centuries in Europe, particularly, the flamboyance of stylized capital punishment was especially marked however. As Johan Huizinga has observed, increasing emphasis on public execution is one of the powerful impressions of the waning Middle Ages.[1] Public execution probably reached its apogee of artful performance during the sixteenth century. The incredibly lurid accounts of the executions of Anne Boleyn, Mary Queen of Scots, and a host of other victims of inquisitional and political terrors of the sixteenth century reveal an extra special talent for making such lugubrious events into unforgettable spectacles. The beheading of Charles I of England in 1649 was one of the last grand public executions in the medieval pageant tradition, and the first under a new system of temporal (parliamentary) law that "detheologized" capital punishment and eventually led to its mechanization and dehumanization as practiced in the twentieth century. Charles's decapitation was to the history of law and capital punishment somewhat as Galileo's nearly contemporary observations of the solar system were to science: establishing that no man had divine right to the center of the universe and at the same time depriving mankind of a convenient human scale to measure cosmic things. Both also deprived man of his absolute confidence in an anthropomorphic God with a master plan of the universe wherein death, even by capital punishment, had not the finality it has today.

It was just such sixteenth-century emphasis on personification and visual impression, it seems to me, that draws public execution into the broad study of mannerism. The tendency in the sixteenth century to insist on high style in matters of violence is almost as characteristic of mannerist painting and sculpture as it is of capital punishment. Particularly noticeable, too, is the remarkable memory chroniclers of the time had for colorful details in recording scenes of executions; details of dress, gesture, and last words. The articulate witnesses of sixteenth-century capital punishment seemed to be more concerned with *how* the condemned went to his death than why he was sentenced in the first place.

This period in history, as John Shearman points out, was self-consciously considered by its own critics as a "more cultured age" than any since classical antiquity.[2] Mannerist artists were particularly concerned with *bella figura*, with elegant personifications of symbols and values from antiquity and the Middle Ages. It was a time of especially affected manners and gestures, not only in art but in everyday life. The phrase "more cultured age" (borrowed from the preface to a madrigal collection published in 1536 by Francesco Marcolini da Forlì) is the title to one of Shearman's provocative chapters in which he takes issue with those who characterize the mannerist phenomenon as fraught with protosurrealism or deliberate anticlassicism. Perhaps, as Shearman implies, we of the twentieth century are too alien to aristocratic affectation to appreciate properly the stylized art of mannerism on its own terms. Following the modern propensity to give Freudian interpretation to practically everything, we are too prone to search for symptoms of our own traumas in the curious forms of *maniera*. We wish to discover in the Reformation crisis of the sixteenth century the *Angst* of our own agnostic times.

However misleading any psychoanalysis of mannerism may be, and it would be difficult indeed considering all the problems of reconstructing that most diverse of ages, some sort of malaise probably did exist in the collective subconscious of the sixteenth century and is yet to be revealed. Certainly there was an increasing acceptance, even savoring, of violence in this era of inquisition, witch trials, and peasant revolts, but at the same time there was unswerving attentiveness to high style in civic and social intercourse. Indeed, stylishness was never more assiduously pursued.

May it not be said that mannerist art was but a manifestation of an extensive and inevitable conflict affecting all aspects of human experience with the imposition of Renaissance ideas upon medieval European culture? Isn't it possible that mannerism was the nervous result of trying to force stylish new clothes on the unwilling limbs of the old gothic body? Indeed, the superimposition of rational Renaissance style upon the somewhat irrational content of medieval mores, as in certain matters of religion and law, produced an unstable emulsion that contributed both to the Reformation and to the advent of a new and strangely distorted art. Yet medieval tradition survived in the Renaissance precisely because philosophers and intellectuals never challenged the substance; they only wished to adapt medieval content to the gracefulness of classical style. By the sixteenth century the Renaissance veneer had become more important than the original meaning of the surviving traditions. Thus, an essential quality of *maniera* was the attempt of sheer style to make agreeable even the most unsavory of subjects, to make what was substantially ugly not only palatable but even inventively fascinating and beautiful.

This emphasis on style over content makes the art of mannerism interesting to critics of modern abstract painting. However, it was the subsequent baroque period of the seventeenth century, not the Renaissance or even the age of mannerism, that inaugurated present-day civilization. Content was again emphasized after 1600, not only in art but in science, law, religion, politics, and even capital punishment. The final eschewing of medieval attitudes during the seventeenth and eighteenth centuries in favor of scientific pragmatism finally brought the West to predominance in the modern world. Regarding capital punishment (particularly in the eighteenth century), ritual, too, gave way to emphasis on efficiency and dispatch. Public execution, which by the sixteenth century had developed into a vicariously experienced and visually attractive *psychomachia* between executioner and victim, gave way to ugly depersonalized killing with machinery; the guillotine, the hangman's trap, the firing squad, and eventually the electric chair, were excused for their lack of esthetic appeal on the grounds of supposed humaneness. Capital punishment in those earlier, simpler times was never so psychologically devastating as it is today. To die in the Middle Ages, even at the hands of an executioner, meant only to leave this world for another. Providing one died penitently, piously, and proudly, there was even a chance for salvation. The ritual of capital punishment was deeply involved with Christian symbolism. To play out this symbolism for the benefit of his soul therefore had the most profound importance for the sinner on his way to death. In an age so concerned with style as the sixteenth century, this ritualization reached its highest perfection. Public executiion not only survived under the impact of Renaissance humanism but even thrived in the guise of art.

Justice, blindfolded and clutching her ever-present sword and scales (as she is so frequently depicted in the Renaissance), cared little about the rights of innocents in the sixteenth century. Most of her attention was given to ingenious punishments. This fact is graphically presented on the title page of one of the most influential treatises in the history of law, the *Bambergische Halsgerichtsord-nung* of 1508 and many later printings (fig. 1).[3] This crude woodcut grimly proclaims the emphasis of sixteenth-century jurisprudence on punishment rather than rehabilitation as the basic method for dealing with crime.

A somewhat later illustration from a French legal treatise, the *Praxis criminis* of 1541, shows the same lugubrious range of capital deterrents: beheading, hanging, and the wheel, all in operation at once in a crowded public square (fig. 2).[4] The objectivity of the scene is relieved only by the foreground figure of a small boy who seems to be losing his stomach. There are many such illustrations in law treatises published during this period, and they may have served as models for Pieter Brueghel the Elder's famous drawing and print of *Justitia* and the painting *Triumph of Death* in the Prado. Brueghel's ironic attitude toward these accepted practices is an interesting sign of coming times. As a northern, six-teenth-century painter remarkably uninfluenced by Italian mannerism, he was one of the first artists to ask "why" to capital punishment.

Such scenes as that in figure 2 from the *Praxis criminis* were acted out once or twice a month, if contemporary statistics are reliable, in nearly every popu-lation center of Europe during the sixteenth century. Public executions were so commonplace that nearly everybody could have seen them.[5] Painters seem to have been particularly intrigued, for they frequently included details of con-temporary capital punishment in pictures of saintly martyrdoms. An extremely realistic painting showing the closest observation of "nature" in this respect is that of Gian Francesco Maineri's, *John the Baptist's Head in a Platter* (fig. 3) in the Brera (Milan). Maineri apparently knew enough about decapitation to depict with grimmest accuracy the anatomical and physiological details of the severed neck and head.[6] Renaissance painters also frequently included gallows in the backgrounds of their pictures.[7] Even such a humanitarian as Rembrandt van Rijn apparently went with his pupils to sketch purely as an exercize in drawing the exposed corpse of a recently executed, notorious murderess hanging up for public view on the gallows hill of Amsterdam.[8]

What particularly interests me, however, is not so much how artists were moved by public execution but how much public execution was affected by art, particularly in the sixteenth century. What I mean by "art" in this context is not just the direct influence of some particular painting or sculpture but more the broader notion of art as sensitivity to stylishness, to an enjoyment of artifice. Since the term *esthetics* did not receive definition until the late 1800s, it may seem inappropriate to use that word here. Nevertheless, *art* and *esthetics* in modern English usage do both convey meanings that describe the self-con-sciousness of style and decorous visual appearance characteristic of the mannerist age. I also believe that painters of this period helped make palatable the un-

B Ambergische halßgerichts

vnd rechtlich Ordenung/in Peinlichen sachen zů volnfarē/allen Stetten/Communen
Regimenten/Ampleüten/Vogkten Verwesern/Schulteysen Schöffen vnd Richtern
Dienlich/fürderlich vnd behilfflich/Darnach zuhandeln vnd rechtsprechen gantz glich=
formig gemeinē geschrieben rechten ꝛc Darus auch diß büchlin getzogen vnd vleissig ge=
meynem nütz zugůt/gesamelt vnd verordnet ist.

Fig. 1. *Title page, colored woodcut, from the* Bambergische
Halsgerichtsordnung, *Mainz, 1508 (Courtesy of the Harvard
University Law Library).*

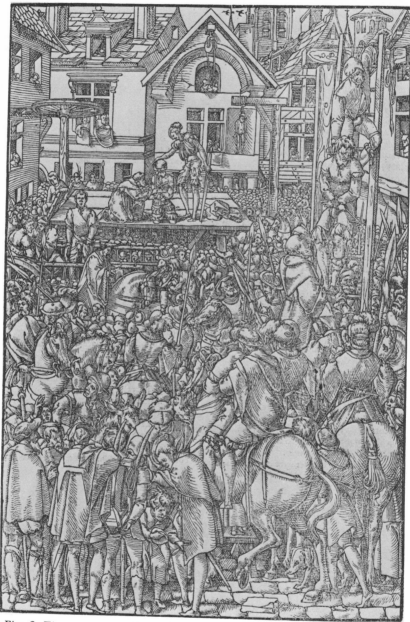

Fig. 2. Figura reorum plectendorum, *woodcut, from Jean Milles de Souvigny (Millaeus),* Praxis Crimins, *Paris, 1541, p. 85 (Courtesy of the Houghton Library, Harvard University).*

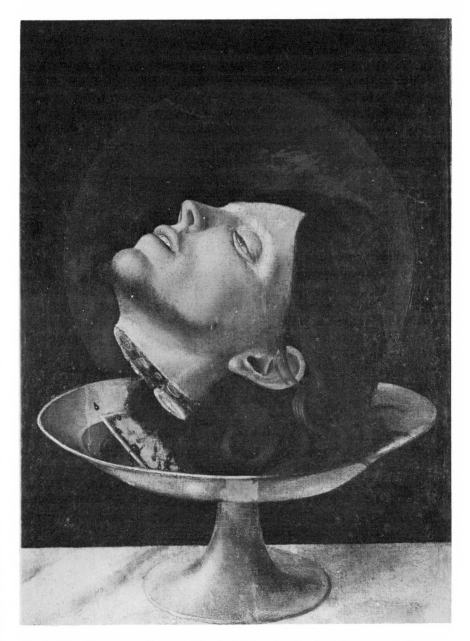

Fig. 3. Gian Francesco Maineri, Head of John the Baptist (*Courtesy of the Pinacoteca di Brera, Milan*).

pleasant social necessity of public execution. In fact, they may even have encouraged the belief that the terrible spectacle could also be fascinatingly beautiful. Certainly the Renaissance painter contributed to making the last moments of the victim on the scaffold more bearable by providing beautiful and beatific models of saintly sacrifice so that he might rationalize his own fate as personal martyrdom. If only to look as penitent and beautiful as St. Catherine or St. Barbara (figs. 4 and 5)! Such seemed often to have been the wish of those about to bare their necks to the sword. Actually, the condemned were deliberately reminded of this relationship by means of paintings held before their eyes as they knelt on the scaffold.

The legal system, as was true of almost every aspect of life in the Middle Ages and Renaissance, was considered an earthly reflection of God's master plan

Fig. 4. Albrecht Altdorfer, Martyrdom of St. Catherine (*Courtesy of the Kunsthistorisches Museum, Vienna*).

Fig. 5. Unknown German Artist, Martyrdom of St. Barbara, *pen and wash drawing (Courtesy of the Fogg Museum, Harvard University).*

for running his ethereal universe. In Europe from the fourteenth century on with the consolidation of urban communities and the formulization of law, the invocation of God's will in legal proceedings was incorporated more and more into the actual architecture and decoration of temporal law courts. Criminal processes were particularly theologized in this visual manner. They were likened often to the Last Judgment with the presiding magistrate acting as vicar of Christ. In the sixteenth century, especially in the trading towns of northern Europe, civic buildings containing law courts were lavishly decorated. Their walls were frequently covered with murals, depicting subjects from the Bible or from classical history appropriate to law. Famous artists were often engaged:

Hans Holbein for the *Rathaus* of Basel, Albrecht Dürer at Nuremberg, and Vredeman de Vries in Danzig.

The commonest mural subject was the *Last Judgment*, usually painted on the broad wall behind the judges' bench. Unhappily, the best examples have disappeared, but the iconography was consistent, following numerous representations on gothic cathedral portals, in manuscript illumination, and on altarpieces (notably Michelangelo's fresco in the Sistine Chapel). A considerably less inspiring print of the *Last Judgment* is illustrated here (fig. 6) from the pages of the *Bambergische Halsgerichtsordnung*. In more ambitious murals of this subject, Christ is usually shown seated in the center of a great arc representing the spheres of the universe. Often depicted below him are angels trumpeting up the dead from their graves while Saint Michael weighs their souls in scales. With his right hand Christ raises the elect to heaven; with his other he condemns the sinful to the jaws of hell at his left. Famous examples of such *Last Judgments* were in the *Rathäuser* of Nuremberg and Münster in Westphalia. Others were painted at Lüneberg, Emden, Osnabrück, Königsberg, and elsewhere.[9]

What is significant, however, is that these paintings of the *Last Judgment* actually related to the proceedings in the courtrooms where they were placed. How this all worked out has been shown by Katherine Fremantle recently, especially in regard to the "new" (mid-seventeenth century) city hall in Amsterdam, which still stands on the Dam Square.[10] The planners incorporated the symbols of the legal process into a *Gesamtkunstwerk* of architecture, painting, and sculpture. The principles of this combination had been established in Holland as elsewhere during the fifteenth and sixteenth centuries. Even earlier it had been the custom during trials involving a capital crime for the judges to sit out of doors, reflecting not only the habit of Roman law but also to identify their role more poignantly with that of Christ in the Last Judgment. Frequently, vaulted arcades were constructed adjacent to town halls expressly for this purpose (fig. 7). When possible, these arcades opened to the east so that the judges, along with the painted image of Christ behind, faced in the symbolic direction of the Resurrection, while the defendant looked to the mystical west, the direction of death. All of these ideas and more were incorporated in the design of the courtroom at Amsterdam. The room let out to the east by large windows, which could be opened for symbolic effect when the court was in session. When the criminal was brought in for trial, he faced the stern countenances of the judges seated under a mural of the Last Judgment and also a depiction of King Solomon. High overhead on the same west wall was a representation of God's Eye staring inexorably down on the poor sinner. Two statues, of *Prudence* and *Justice,* were symbolically placed in the room in order

Fig. 6. Last Judgment, *colored woodcut, from the* Bambergische Halsgerichtsordnung, *Mainz, 1508 (Courtesy of the Harvard University Law Library).*

Fig. 7. Sixteenth century open hall court; *Title page woodcut from the* Neu Formular und Canzleibuch, *Frankfurt, 1571.*

to deter the judges from being swayed by the whims of the crowd outside. At the time of sentencing, the prisoner passed before the judges' bench and heard his sentence from the secretary seated against the north wall, that is, at the *left hand* of the judges. Thus a death sentence was also a vicarious consignment to hell. By means of visual imagery relating to God's ultimate judgment, the power of law and the condemned person's acceptance of the righteousness of his sentence were enhanced. The whole proceeding was made to appear as an earthly preview of the Last Judgment. In Amsterdam, the criminal was then led out the north window of the courtroom onto an especially built scaffold before the building and was made to kneel down, also facing north, before the headsman. From medieval times the north direction was considered unfavorable. It represented the direction of cold, darkness, and death without grace.

From attitudes of the law toward religion, let us turn to some attitudes of religion toward the law. In his great thirteenth-century *Summa theologica,* Saint Thomas Aquinas states that not only is capital punishment divinely sanctioned in a Christian society but that public execution is necessary for the common weal: "Vengeance is lawful and virtuous as far as it tends to the prevention of evil . . . fear of punishment is greater than the enticement of sin." [11] Of course, in those days death did not have the sting of nothingness that it has in our agnostic times. Even the horror of capital punishment could be mitigated by the thought that death was a transition from one life to another, in fact to a life of eternal bliss if the soul were in a state of grace. Since death may catch its victim off guard and unprepared spiritually, what better opportunity than a legal execution for having one's soul put in a state of grace precisely at the moment before dying? While the prisoner by reason of an unusually heinous crime might be denied the sacraments (thereby damning his soul to hell forever), the general practice of the church was to allow the condemned to confess and beg God's mercy as he awaited the fatal stroke. The church's concern was not that punishment might be unjust or overly cruel, but only that the condemned might have an opportunity to save his soul. If the victim really were innocent, his chances of achieving heaven were ideal. "In every case," wrote a prison chaplain in the early seventeenth century, "the condemned ought to thank God for the occasion of dying penitent and absolved of all sin. If the prisoner protests his innocence, he should be persuaded that his death is still very providential."

Even the scaffold, onto which the condemned man stepped as his last mortal act, had a Christian connotation, particularly in public beheadings of notorious personages. Although capital punishment was supposed to be a chastisement and the criminal on the scaffold an object of scorn, there was, in that peculiar "mirror" mentality of the Middle Ages, which continued into the Renaissance, a desire to translate a public execution into a positive religious experience, into a reflection of the Mass, in which the death of the criminal bore symbolic resemblance to the sacrifice of Christ and the salvation of mankind. Thus the scaffold came to be regarded as a sort of altar. For instance, in the little drawing of the masonry scaffold, or *Rabenstein,* in the upper part of figure 1, is unmistakably a painting of the Crucifixion such as might be placed on a church altar. There are numerous other pictures and references to scaffolds adorned with such images of the Crucifixion. There was a Crucifixion, for example, upon the scaffold erected before the *hôtel de ville* in Brussels on June 5, 1568, for the execution by the Spanish of the Count of Egmont and Admiral Horn, heroes of the Dutch rebellion. The scaffold was draped in black, and two rich velvet pillows were provided to receive the knees of the condemned. Plaques bearing the arms of the two noble prisoners were hung up behind the pillows. Three thousand Spanish soldiers at parade rest were drawn up around the scaffold and a provost marshal carried a red baton to give the headsman his signal. The appearance of the two prisoners was carefully recorded. Both were elegantly dressed including badges of their high offices. When Egmont climbed to the scaffold, he laid aside his plumed hat, his Order of the Golden Fleece, and his black mantle embroidered in gold. Possibly these conspicuous gestures related to those of Christ in taking off his own garments at the foot of the cross.

Fig. 8. Execution of Mary, Queen of Scots, *woodcut, from Adam Blackwood*, La Mort de la Royne d'Escosse, *Paris, 1589.*

Indeed, many prints and paintings of executions from this period show details of clothing lying beside the victim. After Egmont and Horn had been decapitated, the spectators are said to have surged toward the scaffold in order to dip their handkerchiefs in the "sacred" blood.[12]

Perhaps the most memorable instance of the scaffold being appointed a church altar was the execution of Mary, Queen of Scots, on the morning of February 8, 1587, at Fotheringay Castle. The evening before the queen was to be beheaded, workmen constructed a scaffold some twelve feet square and two feet high in the great hall. It was covered in black crepe, and a pillow was provided for the queen to kneel upon. In the center was a block, also draped in black. On either side were seats for the two earls representing Elizabeth, there to conduct a Protestant service and censure the faith of the Catholic pretender. The other spectators (invited nobility only) were separated from the scaffold by a balustrade functioning as a chancel rail. A woodcut of the event published two years later in a French history of Mary's execution shows two acolytes holding lighted tapers on either side of the scaffold as the queen placed her neck on the block (fig. 8). Queen Mary well understood the decorum demanded of the occasion and came regally dressed. Under her black velvet robes of state she wore a red chemise with matching armels; red, so she would die garbed in the color symbolic of Catholic martyrs and also so the spurting blood should not stain her clothes unbecomingly.[13]

In Italy during the fourteenth, fifteenth, and sixteenth centuries, religious orders composed of lay brothers were founded expressly to furnish "comfort" to condemned prisoners. In Florence, this group was known as the Archconfraternity of Santa Maria della Croce al Tempio. The brothers wore black robes with faces hooded (thereby earning the nickname "Compagnia dei Neri"). The order was originally headquartered in a little church just outside the Porta della Giustizia, the eastern entrance to the city at the Lungarno, and adjacent to where Florentine criminals were traditionally executed.[14] This church is no longer extant, but the ancient Torre della Zecca Vecchia standing on the present-day Viale della Giovane Italia marks the spot. At the hour of execution the prisoner was led from the Bargello, the old prison of Florence, out along the aptly named Via dei Malcontenti, through the Porta della Giustizia to the little chapel of the Tempio to hear his last Mass. As the prisoner made his final communion here, he was confronted with painted images expressly placed to reinforce his penitence and mystic association with the sacrifice of Christ. The façade of the church was covered with frescoes showing the Passion and the Via Crucis by the late-fourteenth-century master Spinello Aretino. The condemned was thereby reminded that his own "last mile" was a vicarious Way of the Cross. Inside the church, this holy relationship was further emphasized by

Fig. 9. Fra Angelico, Lamentation, *Museo di San Marco, Florence (Courtesy of the Soprintendenza alle Gallerie, Florence).*

the altarpieces. One painting (now lost) showed *St. James Rescuing a Pilgrim from Hanging*, perhaps by Bicci di Lorenzo, but the most famous was a *Lamentation* by Fra Angelico, still extant in the Museo San Marco in Florence (fig. 9). This well-known work of about 1440 shows Christ just removed from the cross.[15] The scene takes place before a walled city so similar to Florence that it can hardly be coincidental. In fact, the depicted distance between Fra Angelico's Crucifixion group and the city gate and walls is about the same as between the old Porta della Giustizia and the spot in the neighboring *pratello* where the gallows stood. It must certainly have been apparent to the condemned man saying his last prayers before this picture that he would be led out to a place just like that where Christ was crucified. As Jesus died willingly for the sins of all minkind, so the prisoner receiving his final rites before Fra Angelico's painting was instructed to accept his fate as an act of divine will and to go to his death as bravely and resolutely as Jesus. Fra Angelico painted other Crucifixion scenes in proximity to city walls that look like those in Florence. In fact, Renaissance painters commonly depicted such biblical subjects in contemporary settings in order to make the Passion more relevant and poignant. While such pictures may have had no relation to local practices of capital punishment, the artists were at least aware of public execution in their own communities and did not fail to take advantage of the obvious association. The sixteenth-century German artist Wolf Huber, for example, made a drawing, now in the Fitzwilliam Museum, Cambridge, showing the Crucifixion as occurring upon a distinctively German *Galgenhügel*. In a somber alpine setting among drooping black pine trees, Christ is crucified alongside of a hanged man and a decaying corpse on the wheel (fig. 10).

The Florentine brotherhood of Santa Maria della Croce al Tempio flourished until the abolition of capital punishment in Italy during the late eighteenth century. Among the similar organizations in other cities, the most interesting and most mannerist in practice was that in Rome, the Archconfraternity of San Giovanni Decollato, Saint John the Beheaded. This brotherhood was founded in 1488 by Florentine laymen living in the Eternal City. Their symbol was Saint John's head in a basin, and their church and oratory are still in existence just off the Lungotevere near the Theatre of Marcellus.[16] The mandate of San Giovanni Decollato was exactly the same as that of the brothers of the Tempio, to act as *confortatori* to the condemned in the prisons in Rome and to accompany them to execution. The order remains today, an exclusively Florentine affair enrolling members from some of the most prominent families in Tuscany. Popes and cardinals have been among its members, and Michelangelo Buonarroti was enrolled from 1514 until his death in 1564. In fact, when Michelangelo died, the well-practiced brothers bore his body to its temporary resting place in Rome (before final interment in Florence).

Fig. 10. Wolf Huber, Crucifixion of Jesus, *pen drawing* (*Courtesy of the Fitzwilliam Museum, Cambridge, England*).

During the sixteenth century, San Giovanni Decollato was extremely busy exercising its mission of servicing the condemned. These brothers also wore black cassocks and hoods to shield their identities, even though their service was regarded as a highly Christian act of mercy. The calling of San Giovanni Decollato is best described by a member of the organization in 1601:

> On the day preceding the execution of justice, this Company is advised, and it sends four brothers of the best disposition. And during the night these keep company with the condemned man, and they dispose him to confess his sins, keeping before his eyes the very bitter passion and shameful death of Our Lord Jesus Christ . . . and they have him kiss the Crucified image depicted on certain tablets; and they keep this before his eyes while they accompany him to the place of punishment, reciting the proper litanies and other prayers; nor do they quit him even on the gallows ladder so long as he is alive. When all is over, they return, in their black cassocks and with faces covered to their church; and in the evening about the twenty-second hour they go with a numerous procession of brothers clad likewise in black, with torches, to take the corpse and bring it back on a bier covered with black cloth to that same church of theirs where they bury it at their cost. They have for their device, the head of St. John in a basin.[17]

To this day one may visit the pleasant Tuscan-style *cortile* of San Giovanni Decollato in Rome and see the flat round plaques, each bearing the device of the order in relief in the loggia pavement which covers the subterranean vaults that serve as tombs to scores of executed criminals. Decapitated victims were buried here with their heads placed neatly between thier knees.

The most interesting aspect of San Giovanni Decollato in regard to our study, however, is the remarkable use to which the arts were put to the service of the Archconfraternity. Indeed, the brotherhood became one of the most important art patrons in Rome. During the seventeenth century, the order conducted one of the great public art exhibitions in the city. All prominent Italian painters were invited to exhibit at a benefit on the premises. But already by the 1530s San Giovanni Decollato had become a haven for work by such important mannerist artists as Giorgio Vasari, Pirro Ligorio, Jacopino del Conte, and Francesco Salviati. The last three painters were responsible for a famous cycle of frescoes in the oratorio depicting the life of John the Baptist. The *Beheading of John* from this series is particularly gruesome. The overall gray tonality of the picture is suddenly broken by a brilliant and eye-stopping swatch of red, representing the gore spilling from the Baptist's severed neck. While art historians of mannerism have always been attracted to these frescoes as outstanding examples of *maniera* esthetics, no one has ever discussed them in terms of their relevance to the purpose of the brothers who prayed in this

Fig. 11. Kusstafeln (*Courtesy of the Archconfraternity of San Giovanni Decollato, Rome*).

oratory before going to attend the sanguinary punishments of the prisoners in their charge. It is to be hoped that research may reveal more psychological connections between subject matter in mannerist painting and the motivations and impressions of the people seeing them during those times. In our era religious imagery and classical gestures have all but lost their poignancy, and it is therefore difficult to appreciate the emotional relationships between particular artistic representations and events of contemporary life.

In this regard, the most interesting of all the applications that San Giovanni Decollato made of art was the employment of little painted panels, the "certain tablets" in the quotation above, which were held before the eyes of prisoners during their last hours. Some dozen or more of these pictures are in the collections of the Archconfraternity. Each is approximately eight to ten inches on a side with a short wooden handle attached to the frame (fig. 11). The subject matter was always appropriate to their use, such as the *Beheading of John,* the *Crucifixion,* the *Flagellation of Christ,* and other scenes of martyrdom. As noted previously, the tablets were held before the condemned to help him gain spiritual strength in his last moments. Figure 12, a drawing by Annibale Carracci (of *ca.* 1595), depicts a hanging in a prison yard. The robed cleric attending the prisoner on the gallows ladder is clearly holding a tablet such as those in the San Giovanni Decollato collection. One can hardly imagine, short of suffering

Fig. 12. *Annibale Carracci,* Execution Scene, *pen drawing (Courtesy of the Royal Library, Windsor Castle, England).*

an identical experience, what the strain on the condemned must have been like during the trip to the scaffold. How incredibly intense, indeed, must have been the empathy of the person about to die with the images in the little tablets held by the brothers. Above all, the pious gestures and noble poses in the pictures were intended to inspire the viewer to assume a similar attitude—a mannerist pose— at his own end. Seeing these innocuous-looking pictures today in the dull show- cases of the infrequently visited Archconfraternity museum, one is hard put to reconstruct the hyperemotion that once attended their use. As his last mortal act, the prisoner in the charge of the brothers of San Giovanni Decollato kissed one of these pictures just seconds before his execution. Thus the Germans have the word *Kusstafeln* for this wholly unique, yet quite unstudied, genre of paint- ing, the sole purpose of which was to provide empathetic inspiration to the victims of capital punishment on their final journey to death.

Who were the painters of these pictures? Those in the collection seem, super- ficially at least, to be rather pedestrian examples of sixteenth- and seventeenth- century Roman mannerist and early baroque painting. One wonders whether some illustrious member of the Archconfraternity such as Pietro da Cortona or perhaps Giorgio Vasari or Baccio Bandinelli may have had a hand in paint- ing them. Perhaps beneath the grime and frequent repainting of one of these little panels there is an original sketch by the order's most famous member, Michelangelo himself.

Of all the forms of sixteenth-century capital punishment, beheading had always been regarded since ancient Roman times as the most preferred. It was generally reserved for malefactors from the upper classes, while hanging, breaking on the wheel, drowning, or impaling was bestowed on criminals of lesser rank. Punishments, indeed, were frequently made to fit the station of the condemned rather than the nature of the crime. In 1635, for example, Giacinto Centini, nephew of Cardinal d'Ascoli, was sentenced to beheading for an alleged plot against Pope Urban VIII, while his lower class coconspirators with whom he had confessed equal guilt were all hanged.[18] The other forms of execution noted previously were not considered especially "cruel and unusual" even up to the time of the American Constitution. Burning at the stake was generally reserved for crimes of blasphemy and heresy; the wheel, for crimes of extreme baseness and for particularly recalcitrant criminals. Drowning was often the means for executing women. Treason, a most heinous crime in those politically uncertain times, was often punished by quartering, that is, by tying four strong horses to the limbs of the body and having them pull the victim apart.[19] While judges during the Middle Ages and Renaissance frequently prescribed extremely painful punishments, they did not confer the sentence of beheading because it was necessarily less painful. Rather, decapitation was thought of as a more dignified way to die and therefore suitable to men and women of station. Hanging was considered distinctly undignified, and hanged victims were often left to rot on the gallows as objects of ridicule.

The very performance of beheading lent itself to esthetics, particularly to values of Christian esthetics. The victim, for example, had to kneel before the executioner in a pose similar to that assumed in saying one's prayers. Hands were bound before or behind, the eyes were usually blindfolded, and the head held erect. The headsman aimed at the vertebrae at the back of the neck and swung his heavy, two-handed sword somewhat in the manner of a baseball bat. The victim dared not flinch lest the stroke go hideously awry. Done well, the head was severed in one blow. A proper decapitation demanded coolness and athletic skill on the part of the executioner and unwavering composure on the part of the victim. Indeed, to die well under the sword was an achievement of self-control that in itself was a measure of one's dignity and breeding. In the entire annals of Christian hagiography, a saint is rarely recorded as having been put to death by hanging.[20] Is it possible that the Christian fathers may even have rewritten the facts in some cases because they could not countenance their sacred heroes coming to such an ignoble end? Most saintly martyrdoms, as any perusal of the subject reveals, were arrived at by beheading. Christian society from its earliest moments was conscious of the esthetic appeal of holy images and could hardly permit them to be associated with anything popularly regarded as humiliating or obscene. As soon as the cross became the symbol of Christianity, crucifying disappeared as a popular means of capital punishment in Europe. Similarly, hanging, breaking on the wheel, and other demeaning and disfiguring forms of execution *as still practiced publicly* rarely were associated with the extinction of saints. At least in votive images there are no depictions of saints' being killed by devices that the medieval and Renaissance European public could associate with the reviling of common criminals.

The block, which in English is synonymous with beheading, was the custom in England and other northern countries but not generally on the rest of the continent during the sixteenth century. Beheadings as practiced in England were often butcher like and repellent to the Italians, Germans, and French. Indeed, Anne Boleyn insisted that her own royal person not be defiled by an English-style execution and asked that a French headsman be called from Calais. The erstwhile wife of Henry VIII was thus decapitated as she knelt at her prayers, with head proudly erect, on May 19, 1536, looking pious and dignified like a queen to the end.

While the judge in the law courts of the sixteenth century was esteemed as the vicar of Christ, the professional executioner, on the other hand, was cast in the opposite role of the devil.[21] In the Christian scheme, God has need for, even as he despises, the prince of darkness. The professional executioner in sixteenth-century society was at once accepted and ostracized. While holding an official and often lucrative office, he was treated as an outcast. He was usually forced to reside in a municipally owned house located outside the city walls, and his children were denied legitimacy. Hence, executioners' offspring frequently intermarried and created dynasties of executioners; which lasted until the present century. Unlike our popular image of the black-clad, emaciated, and sallow-cheeked official electrocutioner or hangman employed in prisons today, the Renaissance headsman, particularly as represented in sixteenth-century pictures, was robust and darkly handsome, a swashbuckling character in brightly colored and bizarre clothes (fig. 13). He seems even to have enjoyed his role of being both feared and hated, the villain in children's scare-stories. He was also a Don Juan and, indeed, is often recorded as operator of the local bordello, or as the "pusher" of necromancy talismans and aphrodisiacs. Among his duties was the administration of torture during pretrial examination of witnesses. In the Scandinavian countries he was in charge of removing dead horses and dogs from public thoroughfares and of cleaning out the town latrines.[22] In England he was sometimes a condemned person himself, having been given a special pardon so that he could carry out the duties of public executioner.[23] In numerous Renaissance paintings showing the martyrdom of saints, there is often the figure of the contemporary executioner. He always carries a big sword, the badge of his office, in a heavy scabbard at his side and seems also to have had a penchant

Scharpffrichter.

Fig. 13. Sixteenth Century German Woodcut, The Headsman (Scharpffrichter).

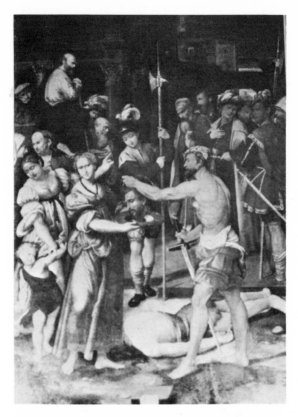

Fig. 14. Calisto Piazza, The Beheading of John the
Baptist, *Chiesa del Incoronato, Lodi.*

for ostentatious plumed hats (fig. 14). In parts of France he had to wear special
colors like a "Jew badge" so that he would always be recognized.[24] During the
French Revolution a minor but positive by-product of the guillotine horror was
the freeing of the public executioner and his family from the prejudice they had
suffered since the Middle Ages.[25] In Tuscany sometimes Moors or swarthy
Sicilians were employed—with obvious color connotations—for this "devil's
task." [26]

In the Italian communes from the late Middle Ages through the sixteenth
century, artists were commonly commissioned to render pictures of notorious
criminals on the walls of public buildings. These were not "wanted" posters in
the modern sense but a deliberate means of humiliating public enemies by showing them in most uncomplimentary poses, sometimes hanging by the neck if
already executed or, more grotesquely, hanging by the feet if in exile or still

at large. This was the practice of *pitture infamanti*.[27] In the Renaissance to have a portrait painted in elegant profile or three-quarter fashion was a mark of the sitter's enduring *fama* and *virtù*. Conversely, to have one's picture painted in an insulting pose, such as hanging, brought everlasting *infamia* instead. Often during the interminable power struggles within the Italian city states, the winning leaders of a successful or aborted *coup* had the losers so depicted. Many famous painters gave their services to this kind of art in Florence, although it must have been a tricky business. One could never be sure that the insulted party might not return one day eager for revenge. Andrea del Castagno, for example, apparently made such pictures of the enemies of the Medici in Florence, perhaps certain members of the Albizzi family whom Cosimo drove from the city in 1434.[28] Fortunately for Andrea, the Medici proved to have unusual staying capacity in Florence, but the painter nevertheless earned a lasting nickname, "Andreino degl'Impicatti" (Andrew of the Hanged Men), probably more in recognition of his lack of prudence than for skill at drawing. Again, after the Pazzi affair of 1478, both Leonardo da Vinci and Sandro Botticelli lent their talents to excoriating the hated conspirators. Leonardo made a sketch of the Pazzi collaborator Bernardo di Bandino Baroncelli, murderer of Lorenzo's brother Giuliano de'Medici, after he had been extradicted from Turkey. The artist showed him hanging from a window of his prison dressed absurdly as a Turk. Botticelli, however, received the larger commission, which was to fresco the whole gang of Pazzi conspirators hanging by their necks or by their feet on the exterior walls of the Bargello and perhaps even on the Palazzo Vecchio. These paintings were alongside of older frescoes showing other, earlier enemies of Florence, such as the notorious Duke of Athens and his cohorts depicted by Giottino after their overthrow in the mid-fourteenth century. All of these *pitture infamanti* have disappeared. In fact, a document still survives in which Pope Sixtus IV refuses to grant peace to Florence and lift his interdict after the execution of Pazzi conspirator Francesco Salviati, the archbishop of Pisa, unless the Medici first remove the unfortunate archbishop's maligning picture from the façade of the Palazzo Vecchio.[29] *Pitture infamanti* clearly succeeded in provoking the wrath of those whose interests they were intended to insult! Indeed, aside from Leonardo's drawing, there are only a few other preparatory sketches that give any indication at all of what this interesting genre of civic art was like in the Italian Renaissance. Some are now in the Uffizi, attributed to Andrea del Sarto (fig. 15). Vasari relates how Andrea was commissioned to represent certain treasonous citizens and military captains who had absconded with the militia payroll during the *Assedio* of 1530. So worried was the artist lest he be called, like del Castagno before him, "Andrea of the Hanged Men" that he painted behind a screen at night and then claimed the pictures were done by his

Fig. 15. Andrea del Sarto, Sketch of Hanged Men,
*chalk drawing (Courtesy of the Gabinetto dei disegni
e stampe degli Uffizi, Florence).*

assistant. The frescoes, which apparently were actually painted on the outer wall of the Mercatanzia on the Piazza della Signoria, were whitewashed over shortly thereafter and, when peace was restored, the charges against the captains either dropped or forgotten.[30]

The fine art of decapitation began to give way to mechanization in certain parts of Europe at least three centuries before the advent of the celebrated guillotine in France. Possibly as early as the late fourteenth century, someone, apparently a German or an Italian, had the idea that beheading could be made more efficient by placing the victim's neck under a heavy blade sliding down between two vertical wooden posts. The knife part of the instrument was either iron or a sharpened wooden plank. In either case the sharpened edge was slammed down through the neck of the condemned by an executioner swinging a heavy mallet. In Germany this device was called the *Dille* (from *die Diele:* a plank, or deal), and the German executioner was often referred to as *der Diller.* The same device with a metal blade was used in parts of Italy during the fifteenth century, as Andrea Mantegna showed in a fresco (destroyed) in the Ovetari Chapel in Padua, of the *Decapitation of St. James.*

At about the same time, research has not pinpointed the place and date, the decapitating knife was simply allowed to drop in guillotine fashion on the victim's neck. Often a heavy weight was released to slide down the uprights and strike the knife already lying across the neck of the condemned. Such an apparatus seems to have been used in parts of Germany and Italy at least as early as the sixteenth century. Several German artists of the period recorded it; Lucas Cranach the Elder, for instance, made a woodcut of St. Matthias being beheaded by this device in his series of *Martyrdoms of the Apostles* from about 1539 (fig. 16). Cranach was not just an imaginative artist with a penchant for

Fig. 16. Lucas Cranach the Elder, Martyrdom of St. Matthias, *woodcut (Courtesy of the Fogg Museum, Harvard University).*

the macabre (tortures and executions are shown frequently enough in his work to justify that impression, however). From 1519 until his death in 1553, he was prominent in the public affairs of his home town of Wittenberg, during the time when the city was the center of the Reformation struggle. From 1537 until 1544 he was burgomaster and may have attended public executions in an official capacity. Who knows but what the protoguillotine that Cranach shows was actually employed in his own political jurisdiction?

In Italy, particularly in Rome, an apparatus of this description was used for capital punishment. It was popularly called the *mannaia*. Contemporary illustrations of it are preserved in prison records of the city as early as 1531.[31] In 1599 one of the most notorious cases in criminal history was climaxed under the *mannaia* of Rome; the execution of Beatrice Cenci, her mother, and her brother for the murder of their father. The *mannaia* also appears in certain sixteenth-century prints by German artists showing the *Death of Titus Manlius Torquatus*, referring to Livy's story of the overexuberant son of the Roman consul who, against orders, advances his troops to achieve a brilliant victory for Rome. But the stoic father condemns him to death notwithstanding, and the subject became quite popular in the Renaissance. The sacrificed Titus, in separate prints by Georg Pencz and Heinrich Aldegrever, is represented as kneeling with his head in a handsome decapitating instrument surrounded by soldiers. The Pencz example is the earlier, from about 1530 (fig. 17). The artist may even have heard about the contemporary use of the *mannaia* in Rome. Furthermore, careful attention to classical detail and the fact that he rendered the decapitation machine as a piece of finely tooled classical-style furniture may indicate that he thought the *mannaia* had always been at work in Rome since the days of the ancient republic.

The tragic story of Beatrice Cenci and her family is best told (albeit as an exoneration) by Stendhal in his *Italian Chronicles*.[32] The facts basically are these: Beatrice was the daughter of a notorious but wealthy profligate named Francesco, who was so base and psychopathically cruel to his wife, daughter, and sons that the family plotted in desperation to murder him. Because of a rash of patricides in the city, the pope decided to make of the Cencis an especially dramatic example. The women were therefore sentenced to the *mannaia*, set up in the Piazza Sant'Angelo on the morning of September 11, 1599. While thousands watched under the hot sun, Beatrice's younger brother, not sentenced to death because of his tender years, was chained to the scaffold and forced to witness the beheading of his mother and sister. The older brother had his body ripped by red-hot pincers on the way to the place of execution and then had his head smashed by a swinging mallet. His body was quartered, and the separate parts were hung on hooks nailed to the scaffold. At the end, the crowd

Fig. 17. Georg Pencz, The Execution of Titus Manlius Torquatus, *engraving.*

surged toward the truncated body of Beatrice, whose youth, beauty, and poise had won their hearts. Maidens, so the contemporary accounts relate, crowned her severed head with flowers. Her body was then solemnly borne through the city to the church of San Pietro in Montorio, adjacent to Bramante's *Tempietto,* for interment. Here she was laid to rest with her head, appropriately (since the brothers of San Giovanni Decollato had attended her) placed in a silver basin between her crossed hands on her breast.

The Beatrice Cenci affair roused greater outcry than most celebrated public executions during the sixteenth century. It was particularly important in molding public reaction to capital punishment in Italy. Indeed, after the inspired writing of the great Italian judicial reformer Beccaria in the eighteenth century,

Fig. 18. Photo: Jacques Delarue, A Public Guillotining in Paris, 1908.

parts of the country abandoned capital punishment altogether. One factor, I think, contributing to the special infamy of the Cenci case, was the use of the *mannaia* itself. This mechanical decapitating machine must have intensified the horror of Beatrice's execution.

In the waning Renaissance, still moved, even in 1599, by the graceful, affected gestures of *maniera,* Beatrice's execution must have seemed especially *brutto.* The public watching her beheaded saw *giustizia* served not by a highly visual vicar of Satan in the person of the headsman, but by a cold and impersonal machine. While the mechanical *mannaia* emphasized the horror of decapitation, it deprived the observing citizens of the age-old ritual of sin and retribution symbolically acted out by executioner and condemned. Indeed, if there was such an artistic state of mind as "anti-mannerism" rising up at this time, then the presence of the *mannaia* added to its definition.

During the seventeenth and eighteenth centuries, European jurisprudence underwent radical change. The concept of temporal law as a reflection of the divine will and of judge, executioner, and condemned as actors in a morality play of the Last Judgment, gave way to a legal code based not so much on absolute principles as in transient public tolerance. Law came to be interpreted not so much by Christ's anointed vicar on earth as by secular authorities such as elected parliaments, leaders dependent upon the popular will, and amendable constitutions. The detheologizing of man's world view in the Renaissance led naturally to a detheologizing of law. The death sentence of Charles I of England, passed down by a peoples' tribunal rather than being issued from an ordained spokesman for God, marks a turning point in the history of captial punishment. Perhaps legal execution has gone into disrepute in the Western world today not because of some special twentieth-century insight that it has no basis in ethics but because we now sense that it has no longer a basis in esthetics.

The reintroduction of the mechanical decapitator called the guillotine by the French in the 1790s finally presented the world with the ultimate horror in public execution. Not only could and did this tireless machine dispatch more victims in a few hours than the best conditioned headsman could in a week, but it did so without any religious sanction, only under the dubious authority of a

Fig. 19. Photo: Jacques Delarue, Louis Diebler, Chief Executioner of France, and His Wife.

Fig. 20. Urs Graf, The Executioner, *pen drawing (Courtesy of the Albertina Museum, Vienna).*

secular and thoroughly fallible state. Public execution in France after 1800, and everywhere else where the guillotine was introduced, was turned from an earthly preview of the Last Judgment to a merely cruel exhibition of man's brutality to man. The 1793 Reign of Terror was proto-Hitlerian in this regard. The subsequent history of the guillotine was thereupon followed by a decreasing acceptance of public execution as an edifying civic experience and an increasing realization that capital punishment in any form is obscene. Nevertheless, public executions have been carried out in the Western world well into the 1900s as figure 18, a photograph of a 1908 guillotining in Paris, shows.[33] Gone, however, is the colorfully beautiful and exhilarating terrible spectacle of a sixteenth-century beheading. Indeed, in this photograph we cannot even find the victim so as to empathize with his plight nor curse the executioner because he can't be distinguished from all the other black-frocked bureaucrats hovering about. It is merely the cold, inhuman machine which dominates, the symbol of depersonalized feeling rather than God's will.

And what of the executioner in our modern age? In an agnostic world, which no longer accepts him as a divinely appointed vicar of hell, he has become the symbol instead of the faceless state, the ultimate Kafka *apparatchik*. Instead of bestiality, he exudes banality. One needs only compare another photograph, of M. Louis Diebler, the second to last in a family of distinguished French *guillotinistes,* seated with his bourgeoise wife in a turn-of-the-century motor car, to his sixteenth-century counterpart in Urs Graf's famous pen drawing in the Albertina (Vienna) (figs. 19, 20). For all the gruesomeness of the drawing's content, the figure of the executioner at least remains a beautiful study in High Renaissance style. Next to his graceful and mannered pose, M. Diebler looks like a piece of Biedermeir furniture.

Our Renaissance ancestors were able, with their appreciation of *maniera,* to establish a high tolerance to life's horrors and absurdities. They accepted public execution as a necessary social institution because it remained in human scale and was done with attention to ritual and grace. They felt separated from the actual physical violence of the act by a kind of moral and esthetic proscenium arch provided respectively by the church and by art.

NOTES

SAMUEL Y. EDGERTON, JR., is Professor of Fine Arts, Boston University.

This paper represents a progress report of a study concerning the relationship between art and public execution undertaken during 1970–71 with the aid of a grant from the National Endowment for the Humanities. The author expresses his appreciation to the NEH and to the Samuel H. Kress Foundation and Harvard University for making possible further work on the project at the Villa I Tatti in Florence during 1971–72. He also is pleased to acknowledge the kind assistance of I. van Eeghen and W.H. Vroom of the Gemeentelijke Archief-dienst in Amsterdam; Ulrich Middeldorf of the Kunsthistorisches Institut in Florence; Goffredo Pucetti, Roberto Pucci, and Dorino Capelli of the Archiconfraternity of San Giovanni Decollato in Rome; and Nancee Singer of Boston University, Boston, Mass.

1. *The Waning of the Middle Ages* (New York: Doubleday Anchor Book, 1954), p. 12ff.

2. *Mannerism* (London, 1967).

3. See Carl Güterbock, *Zur Redaktion der Bambergensis* (Königsberg, 1910); also Fr. Leitschuh, "Die Bambergische Halsgerichtsordnung," *Repertorium für Kunstgeschichte*, 9(1886), 59ff., 169ff., 361ff.

4. Jean Milles de Souvigny, *Praxis criminis persequendi* . . . (Paris, 1541).

5. The most thorough history of medieval and Renaissance capital punishment, especially in northern Europe, including descriptions of hundreds of pictures relating to the subject, is Karl von Amira, "Die germanischen Todesstrafen: Untersuchungen zur Rechts- und Religionsgeschichte," *Abhandlungen der bayrischen Akademie der Wissenschaften; philosophisch-philologische und historische Klasse*, 31 (Munich, 1922), III.

6. Carlo Ridolfi in *Le meraviglie dell'arte* (1648), (Ed. Detlev Freiherr von Hadeln [Berlin, 1924], I, 57–58), tells a famous anecdote about the Venetian painter Gentile Bellini in this respect. Bellini once visited the court of Sultan Mohammed II of Turkey in Constantinople and there astonished the Turks with his realistic painting. However, one of Bellini's pictures, that of *St. John the Baptist's Head on a Platter*, bothered the Sultan, who claimed it anatomically incorrect. When the painter protested, the Sultan called up a slave, had him decapitated on the spot, and held up the severed head to prove that Bellini was wrong!

7. Domenico Veneziono's *Adoration of the Magi* tondo in Berlin, Pisanello's *St. George and the Princess* fresco in Verona, and a sixteenth-century stained glass window in the Cleveland Museum of Art, attributed to the School of Lucas van Leyden, to name but a few.

8. I. H. van Eeghen, "Elsje Christiaens en de Kunsthistorici," *Amstelodamum*, 56(1969), 73–78.

9. See Ursula Lederle-Grieger, *Gerechtigkeitsdarstellungen in deutschen und niederländischen Rathäusern* (Phillipsburg, 1937); and Georg Tröscher, "Weltgerichtsbilder in Rathäusern und Gerichtsstätten," *Wallraf-Richartz Jahrbuch*, 11(1939), 139ff.

10. "The Open *Vierschaar* of Amsterdam's Seventeenth-Century Town Hall as a Setting for the City's Justice," *Oud-Holland*, 77(1962), 206–34.

11. II–II, q. 108, a. 3; see ed. trans. Fathers of the English Dominican Province (London, 1922), XI, 70.

12. For a description of this execution, see John Lothrop Motley, *The Rise and Fall of the Dutch Republic* (New York, n.d.), II, 219ff.

13. See Antonia Fraser, *Mary Queen of Scots* (New York, 1970).

14. For a description and brief history of the buildings associated with Santa Maria della Croce al Tempio, see Walter and Elizabeth Paatz, *Die Kirchen von Florenz* (Frankfurt a. M., 1952), III, 304–6. For a history of the order itself, see Giovanni Battista Uccelli, *La Compagnia di Santa Maria della Croce al Tempio* (Florence, 1861); and Eugenio Capelli, *La Compagnia dei Neri* (Florence, 1927).

15. Documents relating this painting to Santa Maria della Croce al Tempio are given in Stefano Orlandi, "Il Beato Angelico," *Rivista d'arte*, 29(1954), 191, and *Beato Angelico* (Florence, 1964), 53–55, 187–88.

16. Vittorio Moschini, *San Giovanni Decollato: Le chiese di Roma illustrata no. 26* (Rome, 1926).

17. *Ibid.*, 11–12; Corrado Ricci, *Beatrice Cenci* (Milan, 1923), II, 202–3.

18. Giacinto Gigli, *Diario Romano (1608–1670)*, ed. Giuseppe Richiotti (Rome, 1958), 153–54.

19. For illustrations of medieval and Renaissance tortures and capital punishments, culled from numerous contemporary sources, see Franz Heinemann, *Der Richter und die Rechtsgelehrten: Justiz in früheren Zeiten* (Leipzig, 1900; fac. ed., Cologne, 1969); see also Hans Fehr, *Kunst und Recht: Das Recht im Bilde* (Munich, 1923); and H. Ladendorf, *Recht und Rechtswahrer im Spiegel der Kunst* (Berlin, 1938), an exhibition catalogue with an extensive bibliography.

20. A rare exception is St. Coloman of Melk, an Irish priest who in 1012 was mistakenly hanged as a Hungarian spy when he could not speak German to his captors. The story goes that after his body had remained suspended and uncorrupted for a whole year, a hunter discovered it and drew fresh blood with his knife. St. Coloman's remains were then interred at Melk, and he is revered as a patron of pilgrims and unmarried girls. A representation by Albrecht Dürer shows him standing with a rope in his hand as attribute. Except for an occasional picture of St. Colomon hanging and other hanged victims being rescued by saints, I know of no other depictions of hanging involving saints. Interestingly, only such biblical villains as Haman and Judas are depicted in this pose. So also is the vice *Despair* (by Giotto in the Arena Chapel, Padua).

21. For an interesting study of the medieval-Renaissance executioner, see Hellmut Schuh-

mann, *Der Scharfrichter: Seine Gestalt, seine Funktion* (Allgäu, 1964); see also Else Angstmann, *Der Henker in der Volksmeinung* (Bonn, 1928).

22. Finn Hornum, "The Executioner: His Role and Status in Scandinavian Society," in *Sociology and Everyday Life,* ed. Marcello Truzzi (Englewood Cliffs, N.J., 1968), 133.

23. Gerald D. Robins, "The Executioner: His Place in English Society," *British Journal of Sociology,* 15(1964), 234–53.

24. Heinemann, *Der Richter.* . . , 127–30.

25. *Ibid.,* 131.

26. Robert Davidsohn, *Geschichte von Florenz* (Berlin, 1922), IV, 331ff.

27. See Helene Wieruszowski, "Art and the Commune in the Time of Dante," *Speculum,* 19(1944), 22ff.; Gino Masi, *La pittura infamante nella legislazione e nella vita del Commune* (Rome, 1931); Davidsohn, *Geschichte.* . . , IV, part 3, 221–23, and Giovanni Battista Uccelli, *Il Palazzo del Podestà* (Florence, 1865). Since there are no extant remains of original *pitture infamanti,* writing on this subject has been understandably somewhat subjective. The whole problem of political iconography in Italian painting, however, is very far reaching and has been particularly explored by Nicolai Rubenstein in his "Political Ideas in Sienese Art: The Frescoes of Ambrogio Lorenzetti and Taddeo di Bartolo in the Palazzo Pubblico," *Journal of the Warburg and Courtauld Institutes,* 21(1958), 179–208. In the mid-fourteenth-century Lorenzetti frescoes of which Rubenstein speaks, moreover, there is also a very interesting reference to capital punishment. In Ambrogio's painting *Good Government in the City,* for instance, is shown the figure of Justitia with Sapientia flying above holding a pair of scales. In the pans of the scales are seen little allegorical figures representing the two aspects of justice as defined in Aristotle and Thomas Aquinas, "distributive" and "commutative" justice. The latter figure bestows a crown with one hand and beheads a kneeling victim with the other. On the far right side of the fresco, furthermore, Justitia is depicted once again holding a raised sword in her right hand and a crown in her left. Underneath the sword-holding hand and resting on her knee is a severed head. In the neighboring fresco, the so-called *Good Government in the Country,* another allegorical Justice-like figure is painted flying out over the *contado* just beyond the depicted city walls. Instead of a raised sword in her hand, she holds a gallows. This figure is labeled Securitas, a word in medieval Latin which surely in this connection had connotations similar to what certain American politicians of the 1960s and 70s mean by "law and order." All of these allegorical figures relating to punitive justice in Ambrogio's painting can also be interpreted to mean that beheading was a punishment inflicted only on upper-class members of the commune who violate their public trust (the hand that bestows the "crown" of civic responsibility also "removes" it by decapitation). Crimes involving ordinary *cittadini* and *contadini,* on the other hand, were subject to the unesthetic and less allegorical hanging. It is also significant that in Florence and most Italian city states, hanging was actually carried out only outside the city walls. Indeed, one can still make out quite plainly the scaffold and gallows just beyond the Porta della Giustizia in the well-known late fifteenth-century woodcut of Florence known as the *Map With a Chain.* Beheadings in Florence were usually performed within the confines of the Bargello or other civic buildings in order to allow well-born condemned the added dignity of a private execution.

28. Giorgio Vasari, in his *Le vite de'più eccelenti pittori scultori ed architettori* (1568)

mistakenly associated Andrea del Castagno with the Pazzi conspiracy, that is, with an event more than twenty years after the painter's death. Gaetano Milanesi in his emended edition of Vasari's *Vite* has correctly noted that Andrea most likely could only have painted such *pitture infamanti* after the coming to power of the Medici in 1434. See Vasari-Milanesi (Florence, 1878–85), II, 680.

29. Published in Sigismondo dei Conti da Foligno, *Le storie de' suoi tempi dal 1475 al 1510* (Rome, 1883), I, 387ff. The particular article (II, 388) of the pope's edict having to do with Salviati's *pittura infamante* is given below. Professor Nicolai Rubenstein of the Warburg Institute, London, is particularly to be thanked for pointing out this most interesting document.

> *Item cum per eosdem Oratores oblatum fuerit quod pictura, et imagines illorum deleantur de ipsorum Florentinorum platio, ad quod per eamdem Sancititatem responsum est: illud esse debitum, et quod sit honori suo consulere, propterea placet Suae Sanctitati ut cum effectu id faciant.*

30. Vasari-Milanesi, *Vite*, II, 306–7.

31. Rome, Tribunale criminale del governatore, Registrazione d'atti del 27 aprile, 1531 ec. del 6 sett., 6 (Rome: Archivio di stato), excerpts in Ottorino Montenovesi, *Beatrice Cenci: Davanti alla giustizia dei suoi tempi e della storia* (Rome, 1928), 151.

32. For a most unsympathetic view of Beatrice's crime, see Ludwig von Pastor, *History of the Popes*, ed. Ralph Francis Kerr (London, 1952), XXIV, 420ff. The most authoritative and complete account however, is Corrado Ricci, *Beatrice Cenci*, 2 vols. (Milan, 1923).

33. For a history of the guillotine with some, although incomplete, references to its historical antecedents, see Alister Kershaw, *A History of the Guillotine* (London, n.d.).

5

OBSERVATIONS ON THE USE OF THE CONCEPT OF MANNERISM

Henri Zerner

MANNERISM has been a central subject of art historical discussions during the last half century. The term as a historical and critical category has meanwhile been adopted by students of music and literature and by cultural historians and has become the name of an age of civilization. Thus, art history bears a heavy responsibility, and while the art historian might be tempted to drop this by-now unwieldy, cumbersome notion altogether, he owes it to his colleagues to try to elucidate the possible uses of the word and the causes of the present state of confusion. If nothing more, I should like to make it clear to students of music and literature that their difficulty in using the concept of mannerism does not spring exclusively from applying a concept evolved in another discipline.

The debate developed with the partial rehabilitation of the art that separates the High Renaissance from the baroque. This period was condemned as "mannerist" by the seventeenth century, and this anathema lasted until the end of the nineteenth. It was only with the questioning of classical norms, particularly under the influence of an expressionist sensibility in early twentieth-century Germany and Austria, that the situation was reexamined, and at that point the term emerged as a stylistic category without derogatory implications.

I should like to distinguish two trends during this initial period of reassessment. Max Dvořák characterizes mannerism directly in terms of expressive content.[1] Mannerism is defined as an artistic spirituality, and the spiritual explanation of the forms coincides with their description. It is worth noting further that Dvořák is essentially concerned with a general tendency in art, of which El Greco is one of the prime exponents. His views are historical only insofar as he is concerned with the persistence of spiritual values through the sixteenth century, a period when they had mostly been subdued by the materialist rationalism of the Renaissance repellent to Dvořák. Walter Friedlaender, on the contrary, in his famous essay on the anticlassical style, starts from a specific historical situation and a given body of artistic material, namely, the painting of central Italy after

Raphael's death.[2] And he systematically gives a formal definition of the stylistic phenomenon before he attempts a spiritual or cultural interpretation.

After the intial rediscovery, a great deal of work was done to exhume the discarded paintings, and historiography developed along the two lines sketched above. The ideas of Friedlaender gave the impulse for a detailed study of the first reaction to the classical style of the High Renaissance, which found its most elaborate expression in the last chapters of Sydney J. Freedberg's *Painting of the High Renaissance in Rome and Florence* (Cambridge, Mass., 1961). The views of Dvořák, on the other hand, were largely redirected by the rise of a surrealist sensibility, which changed the emphasis from the spiritual to the fantastic. It was no longer the spiritual values of late sixteenth-century art that were singled out and extolled, but the irrational as such. Meanwhile, the term *mannerism* was extended to other cultural domains, particularly by Ernst Curtius, who used it for all unclassical tendencies in literature.[3] This ahistorical tendency coupled with the voraciousness of surrealist taste culminated in Hocke's *Die Welt als Labyrinth* (Hamburg, 1957).

In spite of very divergent ideas, scholars for a long time seemed to know what they meant by *mannerism*. Thus Friedrich Antal, in a well-known essay, could discuss the whole development of sixteenth-century painting in Europe, the relations between Italy and the Netherlands from the 1520s on, in terms of mannerism without feeling obliged at any point to explain what he meant by it.[4] One could give many other examples of the confidence of art historians that, in spite of considerable disagreement as to the limits of mannerism and its historical development, they were dealing with a specific phenomenon. But the looseness of the concept eventually became worrisome, especially because the spiritual expressiveness by then firmly attached to the general use of the word *mannerism* did not seem to fit a whole range of mid-sixteenth-century works in central Italy which were being reconsidered in the 1950s. As early as 1955 Luisa Becherucci proposed to restrict the use of *mannerism* to this art, which we shall call art of the *maniera*.[5] There was, therefore, no longer any agreement about a core of works one could call mannerist, and the historiography of mannerism arrived at a crisis.

It was time to stop, to try to bring some order in one's ideas. Two conferences were held with this intention: the Accademia Nazionale dei Lincei in 1960 and, more fruitfully, the International Congress of the History of Art in New York in 1961. At that point, the main participants, Craig H. Smyth and John Shearman,[6] appeared to have a great deal in common because of their emphasis on mid-sixteenth-century painting and on Roman, rather than on Florentine, developments. I shall try to show that, from the point of view of method, their ideas are divergent, and that the consequences are important in the interpretation of the works in question.

Shearman's effort was enthusiastically welcomed: he fought in the name of common sense; he proposed to push aside the cumbersome historiographic super-structure, to go back to the original sources and see what mannerism really was. Buttressed by an outstanding erudition and an easy and agreeable style of writing, his cause was bound to be heard favorably.

"Let us take it as axiomatic, as history entitles us to do, that every mannerist work must exemplify the quality *maniera*." This sounded reasonable enough; now all that remained was to define *maniera* as it was understood at the time, and all historical complications would be eliminated. From his examination of sixteenth-century texts Shearman found that *maniera* could always be translated by *style*. This concern with style, with the means of art, this "aesthetic ideal" would then be at the heart of a "stylish style," which Shearman in 1961 presented as a current in sixteenth-century art but which in the elaboration of his ideas in *Mannerism* (1967) became a style of civilization.

For Shearman, *maniera* means refinement, sophistication, artificiality, ele-gance, polish, accomplishment, and savoir-faire; it precludes overt passion, violent expression, real energy. Any work "drenched in *maniera*" is to be called man-nerist. Thus equipped, one may easily decide what is or is not mannerist, although some cases are bound to remain in doubt. Most of the art of central Italy fits the concept comfortably, although only some of Michelangelo's works, like the *Victory* in the Palazzo Vecchio, are mannerist. In Venice only Andrea Schiavone seems to be a full-fledged mannerist, while Tintoretto is eliminated by his energy. In France Jean Goujon is mannerist, while clearly Jean Duvet (not discussed by Shearman) is not, as he is too expressive and insufficiently polished. In the Netherlands, artists like Maerten van Heemskerck, although they pre-pared the ground, are too violent to qualify for true mannerism, while the later schools of Haarlem and Utrecht do.

Shearman claims a long tradition, only abandoned in this century, in favor of his use of the word *mannerist*, a tradition starting with the contemporaries of the art in question. This claim is justified only to a point. As Shearman himself notes, in the sixteenth century and in the writings of Giorgio Vasari in particular, *maniera* is used as a critical term and designates a quality, or attribute, of art. In no case is it used as a criterion of a historical period, even though, according to Vasari, it was fully developed and generalized only in his third, or modern, period (i.e., from Leonardo on). It was in the seventeenth century that the historical concept formed: in the period after Raphael and before Carracci, the artists worked *di maniera*, the very basis of their condemnation. It is significant that while Vasari—for whom *maniera* was, on the whole, a virtue—certainly did not consider Raphael or the young Michelangelo as lacking in this quality, Giovanni Bellori and other seventeenth-century theorists did not call either of these artists *manieroso*. The significance is, I believe, not only that a different generation saw something different in the art of Raphael, but also that the meaning of *maniera* had partially shifted. In fact, the use of the word in sixteenth-century writings is extremely loose, in the same way as our use of the word *style* is. Vasari himself does not use it exclusively as a term of praise, for he connects the weakening and monotony of Perugino's late works with an excessive reliance on *maniera*. The continuity of application and stability of meaning of the word from the sixteenth to the seventeenth century cannot be as complete as Shearman would have us believe. Furthermore, with the introduction of *maniera* as a historical criterion, there is an abrupt change in the way historians divide the period, first without, and then with, a break after what we call the classical generation. It is not surprising that Shearman seems to hesitate between Vasari's and Bellori's period divisions. Although he would like to preserve Vasari's terminology and artistic valuations, he cannot help but see an essential difference between the art of Raphael and that of Salviati, all the more because he wants to show that the latter is great in its own way.

Shearman's employment of the term *maniera* derives from his conception of history and from his method. His attitude may be described as an effort to abolish historical distance. He wants to describe the past as it was, to see and appreciate sixteenth-century art with sixteenth-century eyes, as far as possible. Of course, this desire goes hand in hand with a belief that we have more or less direct access to historical facts. A strong Rankian historical positivism is not, however, practicable for Shearman because he cannot claim to restrict himself to events. As an art historian he is necessarily concerned with values and value judgments. "It [mannerism] can and ought to be appreciated or rejected on its *own* terms, and according to its own virtues, not ours." The "terms" are looked for in the writings of the time to avoid introducing modern distortions.[7] I have little sympathy with such an abdication of historical judgment and perspective. Apart from what Walter Benjamin calls the sadness of such a historical attitude, it has a dangerous methodological consequence: while all modern interpretations are held as suspect, contemporary sixteenth-century critical and historical views have to be taken at face value and gain an absolute authority. The art of the period is seen through the declared estheticism and the historical optimism of the period. In other words, Vasari knew best.

But a more attentive reading of Vasari reveals an underlying anxiety. How assured could he be that the wheel of fortune had been stopped or that the biological process in terms of which he understood the development of art had been arrested, that the golden age had come to stay? For him a peak had been attained with Michelangelo and Raphael, and art had reached its limits. His boast that with his own generation a painter could paint much faster is hardly a contradiction, for this is a meager sign of progress indeed. The mixture of bragging and defensiveness that underlies Vasari's writing about recent art—a mixture also found in Benvenuto Cellini's autobiography—hardly indicates complete self-confidence and peace of mind. And when we look at the works themselves, it is difficult indeed to believe that these extravagant displays are exclusively the effect of esthetic enthusiasm and carefree *joie de vivre*.

Even granting that sixteenth-century texts do not demand a more critical interpretation than Shearman supposes, his use of them creates difficulties. He defines mannerism by establishing a criterion with which works are tested and consequently included or excluded. This arbitrary procedure results in some very acute observations on the group of works thus selected, most impressively in Shearman's treatment of what he calls "characteristic forms." But from the point of view of historical interpretation it has an important weakness: it isolates mannerism from all the other phenomena that are tested and rejected, and particularly from the "anticlassical" art of the young Rosso and Pontormo.

Shearman uncompromisingly rejects the idea of a crisis, either artistic or spiritual, marking a break after the classical Renaissance, because a lack of passion or of violent expression is part of his definition of *maniera* and, consequently, of mannerism. Form and expressive content are therefore discussed simultaneously as they are by Dvořák and his followers. Simply, the content has changed to a lack of expression, or to effeteness, and this, so to say, negative expressive content is part of the working definition of the style in question. This adapted *Geistesgeschichte* facilitates the comparison among different cultural forms, through what is assumed as a community of meaning expressed in the different branches of cultural life. The cultivation of elegance and artificiality and even the precedence of the beautiful over all other values are not formal attributes but contents; they do not belong to one particular art but apply to different arts and can define the core of a cultural community. Shearman, in spite of his claims to a factual kind of history, reaches a view of mannerism as a general cultural phenomenon involving mannerist literature, mannerist music, and so on—in short, a style of civilization. It is like standing Dvořák on his head.

Shearman's supercilious attitude toward modern historiography, far from doing away with historical theory, as one would hope, marks a regression to some of its cruder forms. Craig H. Smyth's reticent essay, on the contrary, shows a keen awareness of successive historiographical acquisitions.[8] It acknowledges the direct lineage of Wölfflin and Friedlaender and adopts their disciplined method. Smyth's contribution is most remembered for its concern with Roman reliefs as a primary source of mid-sixteenth-century art, but this aspect of the work is not, in my opinion, the most important. Not enough attention has been paid to Smyth's profound discussion of what he calls the "conventions of the figure." He shows how the artists used a repertory of characteristic poses and

Fig. 1. Francesco Primaticcio, Concert, *chalk drawing with white heightening, Albertina, Vienna.*

gestures to create a rhythmic pattern of angular accents on the surface of the picture. These units are arbitrarily used without regard to the subject of the work.

What Smyth describes is a method of constructing pictures. He has arrived at it by induction through the observation of a specific body of works, those of mid-sixteenth-century painters of central Italy (Bronzino, Salviati, etc.). His approach allows a confrontation with contemporary criticism, and Vasari's well-

Fig. 2. Anonymous sixteenth century painter, Concert, *after Primaticcio* (*Courtesy of Yale University Art Gallery*).

known passage on the repetition of an ideal figure for all the personages of a painting appears as an interesting theoretical justification of Vasari's own practice. The method of construction itself, which seems very strange today, even if we have developed a taste for it, gained wide popularity during the sixteenth century, but it was not universally accepted. For instance, Francesco Primaticcio brought it to Fontainebleau, and his *Concert,* painted on the wall of the musican's tribune in the *Salle de Bal* is characteristic in its elaborate arrangement of arms and legs (fig. 1).[9] A contemporary artist, perhaps a northern painter, who copied it on a panel now in the Yale Art Gallery (fig. 2), felt obliged to give a rational justification to the gesture of the central figure by adding a musical instrument.

A limitation of Smyth's morphological approach is that it confines the discussion to particular domains, in this case to painting. Easy passage from one art to another is lost. For instance, there is great difficulty in coming to any agreement as to what may be called mannerist architecture among historians who attempt a formal definition of the style. Even within a much more limited domain, it is not clear how Smyth's analysis could be carried over from single painted compositions to a decorative system or cycle. Such ensembles, however, became particularly important during the period under discussion, and, as may be seen at Caprarola, a great deal of effort and inventiveness was devoted to their elaboration. One may predict that the attention of historians of painting will turn in this direction after having for a long time concentrated on single compositions, and a serious discussion of ornament will play a major role.

Smyth's painstaking effort to demonstrate the origin of many of the poses and pattern methods used by *maniera* artists in Roman reliefs is not to satisfy an idle curiosity for sources or to show each borrowing as a decisive and yet fortuitous event, but, it would seem, to place *maniera* within a new general view of the Renaissance. This conception, however, he has only adumbrated. If I understand it correctly, it opposes a dominant tradition, with a seminal origin in late antique reliefs, to another classic trend chiefly concerned with "flowing harmony and pliant figures in unity with space." In this view, a large number of borrowings from quattrocento, which students of mannerist art have pointed out, may be assimilated to the borrowings from antiquity since they belong to the same relief tradition. This could also account for the community of forms linking *maniera* art to Pontormo and the "anticlassical mannerism" of his generation. There is a tendency to overlook this community of forms because it is too obvious, especially in such painters as Bronzino or Salviati (fig. 3), but it remains an important aspect of the period and makes Shearman's isolation of what he calls mannerism untenable. Smyth, however, does not confront the problem of this relation. In this respect, one deplores his reticence, but in compensation, there is his strong and strictly handled assessment of *maniera* forms. As for the efficacy of Smyth's general view of Renaissance art, any discussion must await his fuller presentation of what would be the first novel view of Renaissance style since Wölfflin.

In an important essay of 1965, "Observations on the Painting of the *Maniera*," Sydney J. Freedberg adds to Smyth's methical assessment.[10] I do not mean by this that he starts where Smyth leaves off, but that their contributions, although arrived at from different points of view, reinforce one another. Like Smyth, Freedberg starts with a certain bulk of material. The principal

Fig. 3. Francesco Salviati, Visitation, *from the Oratorio, San Giovanni Decollato, Rome.*

question to which he addresses himself is the meaning of this art, not so much *what* it signifies as *how* it achieves significance. Here, Freedberg makes important observations about the building up of tensions among the formal features of the works, the use of quotations from previous art, and the disruption between meaning and subject matter. The problem of borrowings as quotations, in particular, is brilliantly treated. It makes it clear that sources may not be given a historical interpretation without consideration of their meaning or, more precisely, of their function within the new context. Thus, quotations from the High Renaissance betray a difference in procedure and not just an artistic community. In the *maniera* nature is only encountered at one remove, usually through the cultural screen of previous art. This treatment, by the way, does not exclude a keen awareness of nature, as should be clear from some acutely realistic passages, which present recordings of nature more precise or "realistic" than those in High Renaissance works; however, such passages are always caught in a context that points to the artifice.

Freedberg, too, has read the texts of the period, but he treats them critically in the light of artistic practice. And the break with the High Renaissance is reasserted firmly:

The conviction the Maniera painter entertained of belonging to the same gender of art as the first great masters of the "modern manner," was true in part, but it was also a profound and not always perfectly successful self-deception, which the criticism of the next century uncharitably revealed.

Freedberg vigorously reaffirms the break between the art of the *maniera* and that of the High Renaissance, as well as the general continuity between the first postclassical generation (Pontormo, Rosso, Polidoro, Giulio) and the *maniera*. But in these observations he does not examine the latter relationship in detail. He only suggests in general terms that the difficulty comes largely from a wrong assessment of the "first generation mannerists" or, in other words, from too great an insistence upon the Florentine development and its anticlassical, expressionistic aspects and an insufficient consideration of the art of Rome. In any case, striking differences remain between the meanings of different works within what Freedberg sees as the stylistic unity of mannerism, not only between the aggressive estheticism of Bronzino and the earnest violence of the young Pontormo, but even between the elegance of the *maniera* and Parmigianino.

It might appear at first sight that, in the end, Shearman, Smyth, and Freedberg agree on the general contour of *maniera* art: attempts to restrict the term *mannerism* to the *maniera* make little difference as long as everyone is talking about the same thing. But everyone is not talking about the same "thing." Historical categories are not things or natural objects but constructs which are more or less pertinent, that is, which accommodate more or less data and observations. Shearman not only treats mannerism like something that exists (or existed) but also blurs different levels of historical abstraction by using the esthetic ideas of a small group of artists as a criterion for a whole style of European civilization during a large part of the sixteenth century. The most apparent result of this weakness is a misrepresentation of some important works. His book leaves the general impression that mannerism is a sort of art for art's sake, an art disengaged from life and any experience other than esthetic, and that it must be understood and judged as such. I do not think that this is even a fruitful way of looking at the works of the specific group that actually propounded something resembling this esthetic theory. But when it is applied to Parmigianio, it decidedly seems a distortion. The *Madonna of the Long Neck,* however beautiful, refined, and elegant, directly suggests, to me at least, an intense spiritual experience. In other words, even at the level of intention, disregard of reality does not point to the discreteness of the world of art but to the autonomy of the spiritual world.

The investigations of Smyth and Freedberg—and Shearman, for that matter —show to what extent the *maniera* was an art of culture. By that I mean that its conventions depended on a knowledge of the art of the past, especially the recent past, and were not inherent in the works themselves. In the *maniera* to a much greater extent than in early mannerism and the High Renaissance, the justification of the forms was exterior to the context in which they were used. Today's art seems to be in a comparable situation, a fact that would explain why we are more receptive to the *maniera* than previous generations. A work by Ellsworth Kelly has meaning largely because of our knowledge of its place in the historical development of art, because of our understanding of the reduction it operates within that context. Otherwise it would be senseless surfaces of flat colors.

The conventional nature of *maniera* art explains why its meaning was quickly lost sight of. The example of the copyist who misunderstood or rejected Primaticcio's intentions is characteristic. But if this fact explains the long period of neglect, it does not justify the hate and contempt that so often pursued this art. An adequate assessment must account for this distaste, even if we want to rehabilitate the works. In this connection, it is important to emphasize that the immediately expressive anticlassical or postclassical art—in which I would include Parmigianino and Giulio, even though one is suave and the other classicistic —rarely suffered the absolute condemnation that fell upon the *maniera*.

Freedberg shows how the forms and figures assembled in *maniera* are cut off from their original meaning by being taken out of context. The result is that the artist's preoccupation appears totally esthetic, that is, predominantly concerned with the processes of art. Does this mean that those who elaborate on the torment and anxiety of the mannerist age, including the *maniera* proper, are totally in the wrong? I do not think so. The agitated, sometimes violent, forms inherited from the previous period retained something of their expressive force, something of the significance they had either in classic Renaissance art or for the generation of Pontormo. But there was a slight displacement or, if you like, a shift in the relation between form and content. As they became conventional and institutionalized, the charged forms and figures, no longer attached to particular feelings, emotions, or situations, became expressive of a communal subconscious. I do not mean this in a Jungian sense, of a perennial dream of humanity, but, on the contrary, of something peculiar to a given social community. (Clearly I apply terms used for individuals to a social group. But the mapping out of an individual's psyche is an intellectual tool developed by psychologists rather than a reality, and the pattern might still prove useful when applied to a social entity.) I call this collective expression subconscious, because it is bound up with the very conventions of the artistic language; it is attached to the artistic idiom or style and not to one artist or to one work. And it may even be in direct contradiction to a particular work. As such, it escapes the artist's control, although it is effectively exploited under the most favorable con-

Fig. 4. Alessandro Allori, Pearl Fishermen, *from the Studiolo of Francesco I, Palazzo Vecchio, Florence (Photo: Alinari-Giraudon).*

ditions. This part of the meaning of works of art exists at any time but seems to assume a more prominent role during the *maniera*. The rhetorical exaggeration, the emptiness of expressive poses, are playful on one level but also reveal an underlying unrest, an unadmitted torment.

I shall give some examples to illustrate this hypothesis, but only an examination of many works would confirm its utility. Alessandro Allori's well-known *Pearl Fishermen* (fig. 4) is a work of refinement and charm and unquestionably belongs in the art of the *maniera*. The agitated, contorted figures are in contradiction to the generally pleasant character of the scene, the subject matter apparently being less important than the general tone. The whole conception is, in fact, strongly reminiscent of Michelangelo's *Deluge* on the Sistine ceiling (fig. 5), a work in which he puts the greatest strain upon the classical idiom. It would be fair to say that Allori was anxious to emulate the art of Michelangelo, its formal beauty, without retaining the poignancy of the work. The result, however, is an overstatement, which, if we are attentive to it and take it at all seriously, appears a strangely troubling absurdity.

At a much higher level of accomplishment, Cellini's *Saltcellar* (fig. 6), made

Fig. 5. Michelangelo, The Deluge, *ceiling of the Sistine Chapel, Vatican, Rome (Photo: Anderson-Giraudon).*

Fig. 6. Benvenuto Cellini, Saltcellar of Francis I, *gold and enamel, Kunsthistorisches Museum, Vienna (Photo: Bulloz).*

for Francis I, is equally ambiguous. The gold and enamel are festive; the extreme elaboration for so little salt and the iconography of Neptune in such a context are clearly playful. But at the same time there is something extremely serious about the work, in the very expression of the faces, in the heroic nudes so strongly articulated. The violent contrasts of scale, particularly between the two female nudes (Amphitritis and the nude on top of the small arch of triumph), the ambiguity of the sea horses that have the liveliness of real sea horses but are in fact the decoration of Neptune's throne—all this creates tensions that exceed courtly entertainment and the charm of an ornate object. In the saltcellar, one of the most successful works of the time, amusement becomes a pretext and a mask for seriousness. In a reversal of relation, the mock-heroic turns into a very elevated kind of poetry, although the elevation of tone is ostensibly involuntary, essentially unrelated to, and at odds with, both the scale and the purpose of the work.

In the end, it still seems profitable to envisage sixteenth-century art in terms of a crisis and the collapse of the humanistic ideals of the High Renaissance. In at least one other domain a refusal to acknowledge a crisis could not claim the support of common sense. Luther's theses of 1517 marked the beginning of a crisis in spiritual and religious life, although one could show that they were prepared by a long historical development in the fifteenth century and before —indeed history may always be seen as a continuum. The relation between this crisis and that of art, however, is a dangerous subject, and I should not like to venture into it here: on one hand, it would be unhistorical to deny any connection; on the other, a historical interpretation directly explaining one by the other and presenting the artistic phenomena as an expression of spiritual life would be too crude. While certain works may be understood in terms of the religious ideas they reflect, it is doubtful that a style could be explained convincingly in this fashion. The reason is simply that spiritual life itself is not a primary aspect of existence but a form of expression, a cultural phenomenon comparable to art.

The sixteenth century apparently did not solve its artistic crisis. The first artists to be faced by it gave a number of highly personal responses, not only Pontormo and the anticlassical artists of Tuscany, but also Giulio, especially in the *Sala di Costantino,* and perhaps also Polidoro.[11] Succeeding generations appear to have suppressed and masked the crisis by an affirmation of confidence in artistic professionalism. The estheticism of the *maniera* and the reliance on the art of the past are the result. But this confidence in professionalism and in the independence of esthetic values, implicit in the works and explicit in the written theory, this belief that art can disengage itself from life, seem to me no less of a self-deception than the historical one exposed by Freedberg. The result is that a palpable portion of the work's meaning, what is inherently expressive in the forms, appears to escape the artist's control, to be independent of the work's function and even in frequent contradiction to the explicit subject matter. No wonder that this phenomenon, which I cannot but call an artistic alienation, became the subject of profound distaste during an age that was progressively more concerned with expression, with the unity of the work of art, and the central importance of "decorum."

NOTES

Henri Zerner is Associate Professor of Art, Brown University.

1. Über Greco und den Manierismus," *Kunstgeschichte als Geistesgeschichte*, Munich, 1928. For an abbreviated English translation, see John Coolidge, *Magazine of Art*, XLVI, no. 1 (1953), 23.

2. "Die Entstehung des antiklassischen Stiles in der italienischen Malerei um 1520," *Repertorium für Kunstwissenschaft*, XLVI, 1925, 49ff.; trans. in *Mannerism and Anti-Mannerism in Italian Painting* (New York, 1957).

3. *European Literature and the Latin Middle Ages* (New York, 1953); the work was originally published in 1938.

4. "Zum Problem des niederländischen Manierismus," *Kritische Berichte*, III–IV (1928–29), 213ff.

5. "Momenti dell'arte fiorentina nel cinquecento," in *Libera cattedra di storia della civiltà fiorentina* (*Unione fiorentina*): *Il Cinquecento* (Florence, 1955), pp. 161ff.

6. *Manierismo, borocco, rococo: Concetti e termini* (Rome, 1962); *Studies in Western Art: The Renaissance and Mannerism* (New York, 1963) vol. II. Cf. particularly C. H. Smyth "Mannerism and Maniera" pp. 174–199; J. Shearman " 'Maniera' as an Aesthetic Ideal," pp. 200–221.

7. "In the attempt to rescue sixteenth-century art from the ill repute that much of it enjoyed in the nineteenth century, it has been endowed with virtues peculiar to our time—especially the virtues of aggression, anxiety and instability" (*Mannerism*, 1967, p. 15). The idea that such "virtues" were superimposed on works just to save them from disrepute, out of, I suppose, historical charity, seems strange and unlikely to me.

8. *Mannerism and Maniera* (Locust Valley, New York, n.d. [1962]); the text is the same as that in *Studies in Western Art* but with the addition of 58 pages of footnotes. These provide a comprehensive review of the literature and a number of important observations. One only regrets the lack of an index.

9. The painting, executed by Niccolò del Abbate, still exists in the *Salle de Bal* but in a much damaged condition. The extent of the damage was revealed by the removal of the nineteenth-century repaints. We reproduce instead Primaticcio's original drawing in the Albertina (fig. 1). That the triangle was not introduced in the fresco is confirmed by Bétou's etching made in the early seventeenth century. The Louvre preserves a damaged but beautiful painted version, emanating from the circle of Primaticcio and possibly based on the drawing. This painting might have been the immediate model for the Yale panel, which does not seem to have been copied from the fresco.

10. *Art Bulletin*, 1965, pp. 187ff.

11. Polidoro is a difficult case because much of his work has been destroyed; however, his physiognomy has been greatly clarified by modern British connoisseurship and by Marabottini's recent monograph. The main extant painting remains the *Carrying of the Cross*

in Naples, a very individual and in many ways unexpected work. Longhi's belief that a northern artist must have collaborated with Polidoro and painted the main figures is an unlikely hypothesis firmly rejected by Marabottini, but it points significantly to Polidoro's expressive tendencies.

6

THE MAKING OF A RENAISSANCE BOOK

Ray Nash

ONE of the most important documents in the history of bookmaking is the earliest detailed account of printing, published by Christophe Plantin in 1567 and doubtless of his authorship. It is in the form of a dialogue between Jacques Grévin, the dramatist, poet, and physician, and the famous printer Robert Estienne. It purports to be "pour les jeunes enfans" to inform them regarding "this marvellous art of printing" and to cultivate their powers in the use of language, since the matter is set forth in parallel French and Flemish. The account is, in fact, so important that a film illustrating it has recently been made. Since it may prove useful to the readers of this volume, as well as to students of the history of printing, to study the method of making books in the sixteenth century, I have placed photographs made from separate frames of this film next to the appropriate excerpts from Plantin's dialogue.

Rigorous fidelity to the text of 1567 imposed some restrictions on Dana W. Atchley III in making the film. In adhering to Plantin's (or his editor's) mid-sixteenth-century terms he gains absolute authority, but at the cost of oblique patches that can be cleared up only by appealing to Joseph Moxon's *Mechanick Exercises* of 116 years later. Considering the scope and avowed purpose of the Plantin document, however, the student of bibliography is offered a fairly detailed exposition of printing within a century of the death of Gutenberg. No description of bindery operations is included, because books commonly issued from the press to the book trade for retail as unbound sheets.

The author of the film carried through the project from 1966 to 1969. His camera work was done in repeated visits to Plantin's splendid old house in the Friday Market of Antwerp. As a fellow of the American Friends of the Plantin-Moretus Museum he had there the constant advice and full cooperation of Leon Voet, the director, and the staff, and the freedom of the most complete collection of ancient equipment for book production and the most extensive archives on the subject in existence. The project was supported by a Reynolds Scholarship from Dartmouth and a grant from Yale.

The text used for the film, of which Professor Atchley is narrator, is the English translation of the ninth dialogue on writing and printing published in 1964 by the Plantin-Moretus Museum,[1] The second part begins with Grévin, the stooge, demanding of his companion, the master printer, what constitute the principal parts of his art and being told, "They are the types, the form or assemblage of them, and the press." The questions and answers, loaded with technical terms, then come thick and fast, and a valuable picture of the making of books in the mid-sixteenth century is pieced together. The following synopsis sketches the ground covered and gives some indication of the method:

Types and their genesis are discussed first.

"To make types for printing it is necessary to have punches of steel on which the letter is engraved with burins and counterpunches. (Figs. 1a, 1b, & 1c.) When it is done, it is struck into copper and a matrix is made, which is nothing but the impression of the character struck, exactly as when a seal is impressed in wax. Into this matrix the type metal, such as lead or tin, of which they wish to make the type, is poured, in a mould."

Grévin takes this opportunity to ask the printer another leading question.

"I understand what you mean," he remarks. "However, it seems to me very difficult to make that into types so expertly proportioned that they all go together exactly."

"That is done by means of the mould," Estienne responds (Fig. 2.), "which is made of several pieces fastened together, by which all the types are made alike, being as they say of the same font."

Grévin sums up the matter in the best didactic fashion. (Figs. 3 & 4.)

"The mould may thus take the matrix of an A as readily as that of a B and

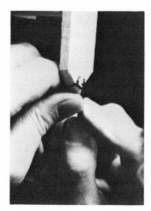

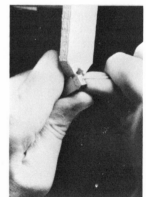

Fig. 1a.   Fig. 1b.   Fig. 1c.

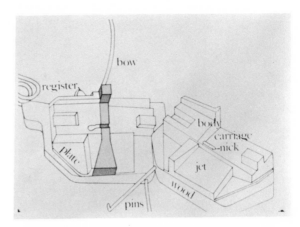

Fig. 2.

Fig. 3

Fig. 4.

Fig. 5.

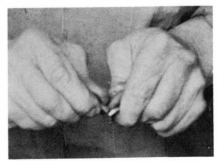

Fig. 6.

Fig. 7.

Fig. 8.

Fig. 9.

Fig. 10.

so on, and the A and B are therefore proportioned alike." (Figs. 5–8.)

Estienne continues with a careful description of this most central and vital instrument of typography, naming all the parts, and again Grévin caps the point.

"This, then, is how the fonts are cast inside the moulds, to which the matrices are attached. But how do you come to have so many kinds of types?" (Figs. 9 & 10.)

"That is on account of the diversity of works that have to be printed," the printer explains, "either in large or smaller letter." And the types have received their names, he adds, according to the kinds of books they are customarily used for, such as missal types, or according to authors, such as cicero and augustine types. Others are named for the nations that use them commonly, such as roman, italic, Greek, and lettre francoise. Still other names are given for great beauty, for example, minion, nonpareil, and paragon as well as for other reasons.

Adding that all types and even the notes of music are made in the same way,

Fig. 11.

Fig. 12.

Fig. 13.

Fig. 14.

Estienne continues, "It should be remarked that each kind of type has its capitals or versals, abbreviations, ligatures, numbers or figures, titling letters, accents, spaces, quadrats, divisions, distinctions." (Fig. 11.) Indeed sometimes the mentor seems overly proud of these long catalogues of terms; if so, the twentieth-century student is indebted to his vanity.

"But tell me," Grévin asks," is everything printed at the press done from foundry materials?"

"No. Sometimes they cut on wood lettres grises and flowered letters, fleurons, chapter headings, and vignettes. And most of the portraits and figures which are put in a book, save those engraved on copper."

Estienne next discusses the form, or assemblage, of types, as he calls the second principal part of the printer's art. (Fig. 12.) Composition is the initial step, whereby the compositor assembles types, lines, and pages. With the question "Then do you print the pages, one after the other?" Grévin elicits explanation of the next step, imposition. (Figs. 13 & 14.)

Fig. 15.

Fig. 16.

Fig. 17.

Fig. 18.

"Not at all. But when he has set two or four or six or eight of them, depending on the size of the book, he imposes them all together in a chase." (Fig. 15.)

The third step, lock up of the form in a chase by means of quoins and furniture, inspires wonderment in the obliging pupil, who wants to know how the types are held firmly in a mere frame, "for there must be innumerable pieces." (Fig. 16.)

"It is true. However, he locks them with quoins in such a way that all the pieces are pressed in from every side. (Fig. 17.) Like the staves of a wooden measure by its hoops."

"I see how that is, for each one of the types is justified in proportion to every other one."

The dialogists now follow the locked-up form to the press, where the third principal part of Estienne's art is carried on. He names all the parts and explains the operation of the wood-framed, two-pull mechanism similar to those in general use from the time of Gutenberg until the nineteenth century. (Figs.

Fig. 19.   Fig. 20.

Fig. 21.   Fig. 22.

18 & 19.) The detailed description points out refinements—for example, the platen is "a large and broad piece of iron"—that seem technically in advance of Moxon's press. (Fig. 20.)

The exposition, however precious to students of bibliography more than four centuries later, is almost too much for Grévin, playing the part of visitor. "But is the paper never going to be laid on?" he breaks in impatiently. Accordingly, the printer describes how the sheet is pricked onto points on the outer tympan, covered by a frisket properly cut out (Figs. 21 & 22.); how the paper must be prepared the day before by dampening; and how the ink balls are made ready, charged with the thick and sticky ink, and beaten on the form. (Fig. 23.)

"The tympan is then lowered, the frisket being fixed, and taking the rounce by the handle the pressman makes the coffin enter halfway under the platen. The bar is pulled for the first time, the coffin is run on in the other half, and the bar pulled a second time."

"Why is the coffin not run clear in the first time?"

"Because the platen cannot cover the whole form," the printer explains,

Fig. 23.   Fig. 24.

though another way of saying it would be that the old-fashioned, loose-jointed screw press could not deliver pressure enough to print off a larger area satisfactorily. Asked about remedies for mistakes in composition, the printer says:

"It is corrected after a proof of it has been seen. The form is unlocked with a shooting stick and hammer. Then the compositor pulls out the extra or faulty types with his bodkin and inserts others in their place. (Fig. 24.) If there is a loose spot, he fills in with quadrats or spaces or broken type. In short, he can easily put in or take out as he likes."

"That is an amazing thing!"

As author and editor Grévin is regarding the printing art with growing enthusiasm. Estienne continues to describe the procedure.

"While it is being done, one of the printers adjusts the frisket and the other rubs out the ink with a brayer and spreads it with a slice so that it will be easier for the balls to take up."

"I see that there are wonderful practices!"

Estienne points out a fact well known to a printer and often overlooked by his customers—that printing economy depends upon mass production. "It is only the first sheet that costs so much," he remarks, "for after that they can be pulled one after another, two or three thousand or as many as are wanted." He then describes the final duty of scrubbing the forms with lye and returning the type to the compositor for distribution, "each one to the box from which he had taken it."

"I should never have thought there was so much to it!" cries Grévin, with all novices through the ages after the first visit to a printing office. "And I am very much pleased by the understanding you have given me by this discussion. However, I must see it actually done, if you please. I have, moreover, something to get printed."

"We will do it whenever you wish," Estienne answers in a voice sounding very like Plantin. "Also you will be introduced to many things which I have perhaps overlooked."

NOTES

Ray Nash is Professor Emeritus of Art, Dartmouth College.

1. Ray Nash, ed. and trans., *Calligraphy and Printing in the Sixteenth Century: Dialogue Attributed to Christophe Plantin in French and Flemish Facsimile* (Antwerp, 1964); the foreword is by Stanley Morison.

INDEX